BEYOND THE HORIZON

BEYOND THE HORIZON

A Search for Meaning in Suffering

CICELY SAUNDERS

DARTON, LONGMAN AND TODD
LONDON

First published in 1990 by
Darton, Longman and Todd Ltd
89 Lillie Road, London sw6 1ud

British Library Cataloguing in Publication Data

Beyond the horizon : a search for meaning in suffering.
  1. English religious literature, 1600–1985. Anthologies
  I. Saunders, *Dame* Cicely
  820.80382

ISBN 0–232–51875–0

Cover design: Marian Bohusz

All royalties earned by the sale of this book are being given to St Christopher's
Hospice, 51–59 Lawrie Park Road, Sydenham, se26 6dz.

Phototypeset by Input Typesetting Ltd, London sw19 8dr
Printed and bound in Great Britain by
Courier International Ltd, Tiptree, Essex

This book is dedicated to all my patients who have taught me so much, and especially to those whose work is included in this collection.

CONTENTS

INTRODUCTION

'Our horizon is nothing
save the limits of our sight.'

Bede Jarrett

Loss of love, of freedom, of abilities, of self-respect and peace
of mind are all forms of suffering that assail us in sickness and
bereavement. We look back on the past and what has gone; we
wake each day in a bleak present and we look ahead in fear or
apprehension. Worst of all is the fear that we will not be able
to go on enduring our circumstances or that they will become
even more difficult to handle and that we will finally crumble.

Yet if we look around we recognize that it is those who have
suffered and come through who have the most to give. It is also
true that this often happens when they do not feel at all tri-
umphant but rather able only to put one foot in front of the
other and somehow come through the present empty moment.

We live in a dangerous world – but it is the one we have, the
way things are. We have fixed laws of gravity and substance
which enable us to work and plan, and trouble comes if they
are disregarded. Wood is hard whether it is the solid bench to
sit on or the weapon of the attacker. We could not live otherwise
and the risks seem inevitable. Much illness derives from our
way of life, our diet and activity or lack of it. Much disaster is
of our own making. We destroy the environment and people go
hungry and poor, unable to help themselves. We hurt each other,
violence and crime are frightening in their extent.

'Acts of God', the title for natural catastrophes such as earth-
quakes and hurricanes, seem to be part of the development of
the habitable earth, so beautiful when seen from space, but yet
such acts can kill or cripple thousands and leave them helplessly
asking 'Why?'

Loving inevitably means loss. Death and other devastating
misfortunes cut short relationships that are more important to

I

us than life itself. Sooner or later we all suffer wounds to make us cry out 'Why should this happen to me?' or, more poignantly, '. . . to the one I love?'

Life is above all about learning to love and most of us have merely begun when we die. This is the main reason why many of us long for and expect another life. But there are other considerations too. Even those who have no faith in the promises of religion know that continuity in change is a consistent pattern in this world. Dying followed by a rebirth in a different form happens in many ways: matter and energy are transformed, not destroyed. It would surely be strange if our life of reasoning and loving should be the only form of existence to end abruptly, the amazingly subtle energies of our minds the only thing to leave no trace. Alongside this we must also set the fate of those who have no chance of a worthwhile life *or* death, whose possibilities are stunted from the beginning. They surely must have the opportunity of fulfilment after all.

The cry of loss may not expect or want an answer but only a silent listening. Often we are merely called on to show that we are trying to understand, even though we have few answers to give and no comfort that can take away the pain we stay alongside. We all have to find some way of handling our own hurts and losses, and a means of carrying on when things are hard. Unless we do this it is difficult for us to continue to open ourselves to the pain of others or to hold together any belief that there is purpose in life. Above all it is as loss is faced and expressed that the way through is discovered and gain comes through loss.

This book includes contributions written or dictated by patients in St Christopher's Hospice who searched for meaning as they faced progressive illness and disability. What they wrote helped many who knew them and, together with the rest of this personal collection, is offered to others in similar situations and to those who care for them. The other material has been culled from helpful reading during the many years of my own experiences and attempts to meet the pain of others.

Some of those I knew had only a short time in which to fulfil their lives. Some of them found an answer, like the writer quoted by Trevor Huddleston in his introduction to *Dying They Live* (letters written by prisoners on the verge of execution in Hitler's Germany), 'I have learnt much in this rigorous year. God has become more real and more immediate to me.' Others have only just held on in a dogged plod through their adversity. But we may believe that none has gone unaccompanied: 'In all their afflictions he was afflicted and the Angel of his presence saved them' (Isaiah 63:9). Over forty years in hospice work has left me with the conviction that the God who in Jesus travelled the way of rejection, torture and death, travels with all his children. And that, surely, must mean every one of his created beings. 'Not a sparrow falls without our Father' (Matthew 10:29), then how much more man, who is, through the Incarnation, his fellow.

Sometimes the journey seems desperately short. It may have been long enough to achieve a goal as described in the life of Tom Dooley, who worked hectically for the Laotians before he died aged 34 of cancer. The title of the book of his life, *Before I Sleep*, was taken from Robert Frost's lines, 'But I have promises to keep and miles to go before I sleep'. Or it may be the outrageous loss of a child; never forgotten, however short or handicapped the life. Here we can only stay beside the unanswerable, gradually finding a way to believe that 'beyond the mystery lies the mercy' (Jewish proverb). The poignant news-letters of the Compassionate Friends (a society of bereaved parents) show how shared grief can hold together and strengthen even though the pain remains.

It is in sharing our pain that we believe God comes to us as the 'Wounded Healer' (Nouwen). As Bishop John Baker writes, 'All the evil ever done has been done to God, because it is a misuse of his good gifts, a rejection of the purposes he set in motion from the beginning. The crucified Jesus is the only accurate picture of God the world has ever seen, and the hands that hold us in existence are pierced with unimaginable nails.' Books are dedicated to attempts to express a theology of the creative suffering of God but many inarticulate sufferers have discovered in simplicity that he is alongside and have found peace in believing that he understands from within their losses.

But a further question may arise to trouble us. Even if we trust that there is a loving God, is it not presumptuous for us to believe that he cares for our small pain in the midst of the innumerable sorrows of the world? Does our search for meaning and strength really have a place in his concern?

Some years ago I attended evening service in Coventry Cathedral. It was already dark and all those splendid stained glass windows were dull and meaningless. Next morning I went back and they were transformed into beauty and design, the same windows and yet completely different. But I realized something else. Each tiny pane had its place and purpose and it was the whole sun that was shining through each one. It made no difference how many there were – it was the same concentration of light for each. So every one of us may be confident in a final fulfilment in the light of God's boundless love, however many of us there may be. His concern has no limits.

That we should have such a precarious existence is a mystery: that its Creator should apparently never intervene to protect the innocent can be an agonizing question, but if beyond it lies the mercy that sees, shares and finally comes and redeems it all, then we can hope for peace and the courage to go on. Our horizon constricts our vision but it is only the limit of our sight, not the limit of the love and redeeming power of God.

THE SEARCH FOR MEANING

This section includes various expressions of a search for meaning in the unfairness of life all summed up in the first poem. The answer to the cry from the Dark Ages appears on page 79, one of many poems in this whole collection which I have learnt by heart; not an explanation but a sharing of the journey into the final light, answer enough then as now. There are several references to the Holocaust and the desperate torture and tragedy of the Labour and Death Camps. Many people have found illumination in Viktor Frankl's book *Man's Search for Meaning* written soon after years in the Nazi camps. It has brought insight and understanding in the development of hospice philosophy to workers in several countries. In the very different setting of tested skill and care hospice staff still have questions to ask.

Some of the entries come from patients who had to find sense and meaning in their dependent lives. They have the ring of tested experience. The extract from Van Raam looks at mystery with faith but the overwhelming question 'Why?' can still remain. Yet a change to the question 'How?' has brought peace to patients and staff alike. There are many such demands and they can open up the way to creative answers. 'How do I help my family?', 'How do we try to understand this patient's problems?' are two such. Best of all has been the release of the beginnings of faith in the love of Christ which is set against our darkness. This is expressed in the short extract from a sermon by John Austin Baker which ends this group of my well-tried resources.

O God, O nameless Someone
   That which contains all things yet is not contained,

Be there.
What is this in me that cares, that prizes caring above all
    material things,
But You?
What is this that feels there should be meaning?
Something through and beyond the pain and cruelty
Ravaging this world?
Is it You?
What is this that is so deeply personal?
That longs for that intimate closeness
That yet can be separate?
That seeks to create, to bring out of chaos
An order that is not confined?
That loves beauty and laughter
And that sheer zest of living?
    Is it You?

And is it You in the darkness of our minds,
    The injustice, the cruelty, the hurricane?
Can it be You in the evil?
Are you buried there?
You Who permeate the universe and beyond,
Gloriously transcendent and yet immediately immanent
Within the minutest particle?
O God, O Nameless Someone,
    Be there.

For apart from You, the ground of being
    And the transcendent mystery,
There is no meaning.
And cruelty and evil remain,
And pain itself is meaningless.
O God, O Nameless Someone,
Help me to trust;
Not blindly, still walking in uncertainty,
But in trust for the journey
In, through, and out of the desert
O God, O Nameless Someone,
    Be there.

P. Thornborough

Down the centuries man has cried out against injustice and
suffering.

WRITTEN IN 780 BC

No man is in the fields,
The forest's stripped and bare,
A few poor faggots left,
And there is none to care.

These men are in great place,
And still they grind the State.
The people cry to heaven,
And think that God is great.
– Is He too great to hate?

translated by Helen Waddell

In the ninth century Alfred the Great translated Boethius, writing in the Dark Ages:

Thou guidest all things to their certain goal
    All but the ways of men:
    Keep them in check Thou wilt not.
O Ruler of the world, Thou hast spat them out.
Why should the noxious consequence of sin
    Take hold upon the sinless?

O Thou, who e'er Thou art,
Thou who dost bind all things in covenant,
Now, now look down on these unhappy lands.
We are not the vilest part of Thy creation,
Great though it be – men tossed on bitter seas.
Rein in the surging of wild rushing waters,
    And Thou that rulest heaven's immensity,
    By that same covenant, steady the earth.

translated by Helen Waddell

For the poor shall not always be forgotten:
the patient abiding of the meek shall not perish for ever.

Psalm 9: 18

MEMORIAL SERVICE FOR THE SIX MILLION

We remember our six million dead, who died when madness ruled the world and evil dwelt on earth. We remember those we knew, and those whose very name is lost.

We mourn for all that died with them; their goodness and their wisdom, which could have saved the world and healed so many wounds. We mourn for the genius and the wit that died, the learning and the laughter that were lost. The world has become a poorer place and our hearts become cold as we think of the splendour that might have been.

We stand in gratitude for their example of decency and goodness. They are like candles which shine out from the darkness of those years, and in their light we know what goodness is – and evil.

We salute those men and women who were not Jews, who had the courage to stand outside the mob and suffer with us. They, too, are Your witnesses, a source of hope when we despair.

Because of our people's suffering, may such times never come again, and may their sacrifice not be in vain. In our daily fight against cruelty and prejudice, against tyranny and persecution, their memory gives us strength and leads us on.

In silence we remember those who sanctified His name on earth.

Forms of Prayer for Jewish Worship

Even in the death camps men still searched for a meaning in their lives and in their deaths. Viktor Frankl quotes from

Nietzsche, 'He who has a *why* to his life can bear with almost any *how*.' He also writes:

> The experiences of camp life show that man does have a choice of action. There were enough examples, often of a heroic nature, which proved that apathy could be overcome, irritability suppressed. Man *can* preserve a vestige of spiritual freedom, of independence of mind, even in such terrible conditions of psychic and physical stress.
>
> We who lived in concentration meditation camps can remember the men who walked through the huts comforting others, giving away their last piece of bread. They may have been few in number, but they offer sufficient proof that everything can be taken from a man but one thing: the last of the human freedoms – to choose one's attitudes in any given set of circumstances, to choose one's own way.

Viktor Frankl

For us, as prisoners, these thoughts were not speculations far removed from reality. They were the only thoughts that could be of help to us. They kept us from despair, even when there seemed to be no chance of coming out of it alive. Long ago we had passed the stage of asking what was the meaning of life, a naive query which understands life as the attaining of some aim through the active creation of something of value. For us, the meaning of life embraced the wider cycles of life and death, of suffering and of dying.

Viktor Frankl

ENID'S MEDITATION

Enid fought her way to peace and we often had to battle alongside her. She found her profound dependence hard to bear and could be difficult and demanding. Such struggles towards acceptance are often prolonged, as the same battle is fought over and over again and never seems to be finished. She asked sometimes angry but honest questions of the God she deeply believed in and had served during her active life, and after a long battle she gradually accepted the reality of what was happening and found the answer which she has left us, dictated during the month before she died.

A friend and I were considering life and its purpose. I said, even with increasing paralysis and loss of speech, I believed there was a purpose for my life, but I was not sure what it was at that particular time. We agreed to pray about it for a week. I was then sure that my present purpose is simply to receive other people's prayers and kindness and to link together all those who are lovingly concerned about me, many of whom are unknown to one another. After a while my friend said: 'It must be hard to be the wounded Jew when, by nature, you would rather be the Good Samaritan.'

It is hard: it would be unbearable were it not for my belief that the wounded man and the Samaritan are inseparable. It was the helplessness of the one that brought out the best in the other and linked them together.

In reflecting on the parable, I am particularly interested in the fact that we are not told the wounded man recovered. I have always assumed that he did, but now it occurs to me that even if he did not recover, the story will still stand as a perfect example of true neighbourliness. You will remember the story concludes with the Samaritan asking the innkeeper to take care of the man, but he assures him of his own continuing interest and support: so, the innkeeper becomes linked.

If, as my friend suggested, I am cast in the role of the wounded man, I am not unmindful of the modern day counterparts of the Priest and Levite, but I am overwhelmed by the kindness of so many 'Samaritans'. There are those who, like you, have been praying for me for a long time and constantly reassure me of continued interest and support. There are many others who have come into my life – people I would never have met had I not been in need, who are now being asked to take care of me. I like to think that all of us have been linked together for a purpose which will prove a means of blessing to us all.

Enid Henke

Another patient with paralysis who suffered keenly all the humiliations of loss and dependence found an unexpected freedom and fellowship there and came close to God in the end. He came to the Poetry Workshop where others had to read his poems for him.

SMOKE RINGS

I can't blow smoke rings any more:
    My tongue, it will not budge,
But other people's various powers
    I never would begrudge.

It's not for me to jealous be
    And make a silly fuss.
If everybody were like me
    Then who'd look after us?

The more I lose my little skills,
    The more I see God's plan,
I see what really counts with Him:
    The essence of a man.

James Haylock Eyre

PRAYER

I find prayer so powerful
That I need but one:
Heavenly Father
Grant me the wisdom
To see the good
In everyone
And everything.
You know my needs:
I do not need to ask.
I appreciate your gifts.
Amen.

James Haylock Eyre

FALL

Pride went before
– I fell –
Pride went

James Haylock Eyre

O Lord, thou knowest; remember me and visit me.

Jeremiah 15: 15

You order all things graciously.
   You are the mystery
Unfolding cosmos and humanity.
You are my homeland,
My most original ground.
Your Presence
Welds all things together.
You are the caring love
That carries me
Like mother earth
Does forest, flower, tree.
Outside you
The world is a wilderness.
The universe indifferent,
The earth a barren planet
And I a speck of dust.
Your Presence alone
Is lasting home;
You are the Beyond
In the midst of daily life,
The sacrament of everydayness:
Immersion in daily duty
As flowing from your hand
Is homecoming to you.

A. Van Kaam

What was really needed was a fundamental change in our attitude towards life. We had to learn ourselves, and, furthermore, we had to teach the despairing men, that it did not really matter what we expected from life, but rather what life expected from us. We needed to stop asking about the meaning of life, and instead to think of ourselves as those who were being questioned by life – daily and hourly. Our answer must consist, not in talk and meditation, but in right action and in right conduct. Life ultimately means taking the responsibility to find the right answer to its problems and to fulfil the tasks which it constantly sets for each individual.

These tasks, and therefore the meaning of life, differ from man to man, and from moment to moment. Thus it is impossible to define the meaning of life in a general way. Questions about the meaning of life can never be answered by sweeping statements. 'Life' does not mean something vague, but something very real and concrete, just as life's tasks are also very real and concrete.

Viktor Frankl

Again and again, when men have been wandering in a nightmare of thick darkness, they come back to the light of Christ. Christ gives the clear, unshadowed light by which we may know the truth of human affairs, not because he expounded unheard of ideas – most of what he taught is common to what is universally best in human moral insight – but because he never deviated from his vision, he never thought or pretended that the end could justify the means.

But there is one other thing which makes the divine daylight, radiating from Christ, different from all other lights. It is not a cold light of truth and judgement alone; it is a warm and healing light of forgiveness. None of us need be afraid to come out of our darkness into the light of Christ, for that light is not condemnation but compassion and new creation. 'Awake thou that sleepest and arise from the dead, and Christ shall give thee light.' It is perhaps the supreme vocation of the Church to be the place where no man need be afraid of his own life, but where love helps us all to come out of the dark.

John Austin Baker

2

ANGER, GUILT AND FORGIVENESS

Some people are afraid of their anger, especially if they feel it can only be directed at God. I certainly found it difficult to acknowledge or express my feelings in that way as I considered the unfairness I felt and saw around me. Zohar, one of several Jewish writers in this section, makes the important distinction between cries for vengeance, a prayer not answered save by a 'No' (' "Vengeance is mine, I will repay", saith the Lord.' Romans 12: 19) and those of entreaty, which we can make as desperately as the occasion demands.

The Psalms give us many words for complaint and question so it is not surprising that this section should begin with Jewish writers. Rabbi Kushner's book *When Bad Things Happen to Good People* has met the need of many who suffer or watch others suffering, although a Christian would want to go further into God's sharing in the wrongs and mysteries of our pains and losses. Bernard Clements points to this in the extract which conveys so much in a short span. H. M. Prescott, in the longer extract from her powerfully theological novel *The Man On A Donkey*, gives a wonderfully reassuring approach to our anger with ourselves as we look at our failures. And what is judgement but a setting of things right, an understanding presented by C. S. Lewis as he looks at the Psalms. I include here, and again later, extracts from some young Lithuanian prisoners in Siberia. They were not angry but cried out from deep deprivation and injustice as did many of the Psalmists. The copy I have of their little book is well worn.

So on to forgiveness and salvation with a fresh look at these from John Austin Baker's Lent Book of some years ago, followed perhaps surprisingly by Shakespeare himself. The other writers quoted have also stood the test of time and much re-reading and seemed to fit this section.

Finally, to a very different slant on forgiveness from one of our patients. Brenda Dawson was a primary school headmistress who spent many weeks in St Christopher's Hospice facing the challenges of intermittently recurring disease. She fought for independence of body and spirit and, in asking questions of God, challenged us as well. Her last poem on page 23 speaks of 'the new life rising within us'. The poem quoted here was written in the midst of battle, but a battle fought without bitterness. It is a fitting end to this section.

What do we do with our anger when we have been hurt? The goal, if we can achieve it, would be to *be angry at the situation*, rather than at ourselves, or at those who might have prevented it or are close to us trying to help us, or at God who let it happen. Getting angry at ourselves makes us depressed.

Being angry at other people scares them away and makes it harder for them to help us. Being angry at God erects a barrier between us and all the sustaining, comforting resources of religion that are there to help us at such times. But being angry at the situation, recognizing it as something rotten, unfair, and totally undeserved, shouting about it, denouncing it, crying over it, permits us to discharge the anger which is a part of being hurt, without making it harder for us to be helped.

Harold Kushner

Not all tears come before the King. Sullen tears, and tears accompanying the petition for vengeance do not ascend on high. But tears of entreaty and penitence, and tears beseeching relief, cleave the very heavens, open the portals and ascend to the King of kings.

Zohar
Forms of Prayer for Jewish Worship

We do not even know how we are supposed to pray. All we do is call for help because of the need of the moment. But what the soul intends is spiritual need, only we are not able to express what the soul means. That is why we do not merely ask God to hear our call for help, but also beg Him who knows what is hidden, to hear the silent cry of the soul.

Chasidic
Forms of Prayer for Jewish Worship

What happens is that the quality of depression deepens our sense of unworthiness, our sense of badness and isolation. We interpret this as a distancing from God, instead of sheer human need that wants God more than ever.

You *never* lose the love of God, you never lose the love of your parents. Temporarily you are out of touch with one another, and guilt is the warning of that. It should do nothing to your basic goodness or to your self-esteem.

The Church has done something that is seriously wrong. It has confused this signal of God's continuous love for us with making a person feel totally bad and unworthy. Nowhere in the Bible is there the message that sin alienates man completely from God. But Christianity has failed abysmally to help people realise that when they feel guilty they do not have to reject themselves totally as bad.

Jack Dominian

If we confess our sins, he is faithful and just, and will forgive our sins and cleanse us from all unrighteousness.

1 John 1: 9

THE FOURTH WORD

And at the ninth hour Jesus cried with a loud voice, *'Eloi, Eloi, lama sabachtani?'* which means 'My God, my God, why have you forsaken me?'

In this fourth word from the cross Christ went into the lowest depths to which man comes. There he laid himself as a foundation by which we may pass over – like a man laying concrete across a swamp ... However great the depth of sorrow or shame you or I may be in, it is not bottomless. He went lower still – so that we might pass over.

Bernard Clements

Once he had seen his sin as a thing that clung close as his shadow clung to his heels; now he knew that it was the very stuff of his soul. Never could he, a leaking bucket not to be mended, retain God's saving Grace, however freely outpoured. Never could he, that heavy lump of sin, do any other than sink, and sink again, however often Christ, walking on the waves, should stretch His hand to lift and bring him safe.

He did not know that though the bucket be leaky it matters not at all when it is deep in the deep sea; and the water both without it and within. He did not know, because he was too proud to know that a man must endure to sink and sink again, but always crying upon God, never for shame ceasing to cry, until the day when he shall find himself lifted by the bland swell of that power, inward, secret, as little to be known as to be doubted, the power of omnipotent grace in tranquil, irresistible operation.

H. F. M. Prescott

It was therefore with great surprise that I first noticed how the Psalmists talk about the judgements of God. They talk like this; 'O let the nations rejoice and be glad, for thou shalt judge the folk righteously' (67: 4), 'Let the field be joyful . . . all the trees of the wood shall rejoice before the Lord, for he cometh, for he cometh to judge the earth' (96: 12, 13). Judgement is apparently an occasion of universal rejoicing. People ask for it: 'Judge me, O Lord my God, according to thy righteousness' (35: 24).

The reason for this soon becomes very plain. The ancient Jews, like ourselves, think of God's judgement in terms of an earthly court of justice. The difference is that the Christian pictures the case to be tried as a criminal case with himself in the dock; the Jew pictures it as a civil case with himself as the plaintiff. The one hopes for acquittal, or rather for pardon; the other hopes for a resounding triumph with heavy damages. Hence he prays 'judge my quarrel', or 'avenge my cause' (35: 23). We need not therefore be surprised if the Psalms, and the Prophets, are full of the longing for judgement, and regard the announcement that 'judgement' is coming as good news. Hundreds and thousands of people who have been stripped of all they possess and who have the right entirely on their side will at last be heard. Of course they are not afraid of judgement. They know their case is unanswerable – if only it could be heard. When God comes to judge, at last it will.

C. S. Lewis

This prayer and others following come from a book written by four Lithuanian girls imprisoned for their faith in Northern Siberia. Only 2 × 3 inches in size, it was smuggled out of camp with this inscription:

Frances,
We send this prayer book to you in order that you may be able better to feel, think and worship the Lord together with us. Lione made it, Vale drew it, Leonte glued it together and I wrote it.   Ad(ele)

JESUS FALLS THE THIRD TIME

Depressing despair,
boundless anguish of soul,
crushing fatigue of body,
powerlessness of old age
pinion the wings of soaring spiritual flights.

Lithuanian Prisoners

PRAYER

Dead-tired Jesus, help me and my dear ones to endure patiently the helpless weakness of our souls and bodies.

Lithuanian Prisoners

————

When Christ said 'I was in prison and you visited me', he did not draw a distinction between the guilty and the innocent.

Pope John Paul II

It is all grace. It is not even that there is a door which Christ has unbolted, and we, standing outside it, have to stretch out our hand, lift the latch, and walk through. We are already inside. When our Saviour became man and undid the sin of Adam, he did not command the cherubim with the flaming sword to return to heaven so that we could re-enter Eden. He picked up the walls of Eden and carried them to the farthest edge of Ocean, and there set them up so that they now girdle the whole world. All we are asked to do is open our eyes and recognize where we are. Once we have done that, then we shall look down at ourselves and our filthy bodies and our tattered clothes, and we shall say, 'I am not fit to be here, in Paradise'; and we shall ask for baptism to wash us clean, and for the white robe of chrism to clothe us in the righteousness of the Lord. But not in order that we may be saved – simply because this is fitting for those who have been saved.

John Austin Baker

> He died that we might be forgiven.
> He died to make us good;
> That we might go at last to Heaven,
> Saved by his precious blood.

This is the shortest and also the most classic statement of the doctrine of the Atonement, but on the question of how His death procures these benedictions and deliverances for us through all the centuries of time, the most elaborate poetry (of which there is but little) takes us no further than the few pregnant lines which Shakespeare gives to Isabella in 'Measure For Measure':

> Alas, alas!
> Why, all the Souls that were, were forfeit once,
> And He that might the vantage best have took
> Found out the remedy: how would you be,
> If He, which is the top of judgement, should
> But judge you as you are? O' think on that,
> And mercy then will breathe within your lips,
> Like one new made

Roger Lloyd

LOVE (III)

> Love bade me welcome: yet my soul drew back,
>   Guiltie of dust and sinne.
> But quick-ey'd Love, observing me grow slack
>   From my first entrance in,
> Drew nearer to me, sweetly questioning,
>   If I lack'd any thing.

A guest, I answer'd, worthy to be here:
    Love said, You shall be he.
I the unkinde, ungratefull? Ah my deare,
    I cannot look on thee.
Love took my hand, and smiling did reply,
    Who made the eyes but I?

Truth Lord, but I have marr'd them: let my shame
    Go where it doth deserve.
And know you not, sayes Love, who bore the blame?
    My deare, then I will serve.
You must sit down, sayes Love, and taste my meat:
    So I did sit and eat.

                                        George Herbert

It seems to me that the key to this is that God's only power
is love-in-the-form-of-grace – not coercion, not the threat
of hell-fire, not tinkering with the laws of Nature; and
that love is easily rejected. Accepted, it is unconquerable.
But the essence of the human condition, as the Christian
faith interprets it, is that while we cannot escape God's
love (it is offered freely and unconditionally to everyone)
we are also free to refuse to respond to it. God, then, is
trying to be active in every second of history, and in every
glimpse and gesture of Nature. But most of the time man
frustrates Him. God, maddeningly, refuses to hit back;
carries on loving.

                                        Gerald Priestland

Wilt thou not yield me vision,
Lord of grace,
Of that vast realm
Of unhorizoned space
Which is thy heart
That heart-room makes for all?

                            Alistair Maclean

Even though the day be laden and my task dreary and my strength small, a song keeps singing in my heart. For I know that I am thine.

I am part of thee. Thou art kin to me and all my times are in thy hand.

Alistair Maclean

FORGIVENESS

God, you need to ask my forgiveness,
Your world is full of mistakes.
Some cells, like weeds in the garden
Are growing in the wrong place.
And we your children
Have polluted our environment.
Why did you let it happen God?
We prayed with faith, hope, love,
We perceived no change in our bodies or environment,
We are made sick by your world.
God you need to ask my forgiveness.
Was this why you sent your Son?

Brenda Dawson

3

SUFFERING

There is no one path that I have found to help me towards acceptance of the mystery of suffering but several of the contributions to this section have brought some light into the darkness. In their very different ways Teilhard de Chardin's picture of the overall plan of the universe with all the dangers of its development, Margaret Torrie's journey along the Via Dolorosa and Levi Yitzchak's request to know what his moment of suffering demands of him, have all been illuminating at various times.

There are three prayers from the Lithuanian prisoners. They are included because their use has been a way of sharing with innocent prisoners everywhere. The awareness of our common belonging to the whole shabby company of those enduring deprivation of any kind has always held comfort for me. The same thought leads on to the transformation of suffering presented by George Appleton and the others that follow. And that transformation comes from the presence of Christ both within and alongside the suffering community.

The airman's meeting with Christ on the way to the Cross pictured by Dorothy Sayers comes from her powerful play on the problem of suffering, 'The Just Vengeance', read and re-read many times over the years. The quotation from John Austin Baker has borne constant repetition as does Julian of Norwich's more famous phrases.

A constant theme throughout this section has been Christ's sharing and therefore transformation of suffering so that it becomes 'fruitful for God' according to the prayer of the First World War. 'The undefeated heart of weakness', as John Taylor expresses it, will outlast all else and give enough answer to trust and live by.

Over the centuries an all-embracing plan seems in truth to be unfolding around us. Something is afoot in the universe, some issue is at stake, which cannot be better described than as a process of gestation and birth; the birth of the spiritual reality formed by the souls of men and by the matter which they bear along with them. Laboriously, through the medium and by virtue of human activity, the new earth is gathering its forces, emerging and purifying itself. No, we are not like the blooms in a bunch of flowers, but rather the leaves and blossoms of some great tree on which all things appear in due season and due place, in time with and at the behest of the All.

In a bunch of flowers it would be surprising to find imperfect or sickly blooms, because they have been picked one by one and assembled with art. On a tree, by contrast, which has had to fight the internal hazards of its own growth, and the external hazards of rough weather, the broken branches, the bruised blossoms and the shrivelled, sickly or faded flowers are in their rightful place; they reflect the amount of difficulty which the trunk which bears them has undergone before attaining its growth.

The world, looked at empirically on our scale, is an immense groping, an immense search, an immense attack; it can only progress at the cost of many failures and many casualties. The sufferers, whatever the nature of their suffering, are the reflection of this austere but noble condition. They are not useless and diminished elements. They are merely those who pay the price of universal progress and triumph. They are the ones who have fallen on the field of honour.

Teilhard de Chardin

Do not make the mistake
of imagining that you
may go singing
on the Via Dolorosa;
neither may you
bear right or left –
the way is confined
with little room
for manoeuvre.

You will know exhaustion
kneeling often;
trodden and rough
and scarred by many feet
this way is our way
and may not be shunned,
turned from
or avoided –
best to go quietly
with dogged courage
knowing that
one thing is certain –
There is an end.

And when you arrive
you will find
that the hill is crowned
with a living tree
stretching out
great branches
to give you shelter
and manna there
and spring water

Margaret Torrie

I do not beg You to reveal to me the secret of Your ways
– I could not bear it. But show me one thing; show it to
me more clearly and more deeply: show me what this,
which is happening at this very moment, means to me,
what it demands of me, what You, Lord of the world, are

telling me by way of it. Ah, it is not why I suffer, that I wish to know, but only whether I suffer for Your sake.

Levi Yitzchak of Berditchev
Forms of Prayer for Jewish Worship

OFFERING

O Lord, because of Your greatest love,
You descended from heaven and walked
the paths of this earth doing good.
You have endured most painful sufferings
in soul and in body.
You have chosen me
to walk the road of the elect.
I wish to follow You, O Lord,
only lead me, give me
strength and wisdom,
and brighten my desires.
With a grateful heart,
I shall accept all from Your hands:
powerlessness, endless longing,
contempt, neglect and disregard,
the loss of those dearest to me
and of my liberty.
Lord, do with me
whatever You desire;
only have compassion on my nation
and on my beloved ones.

Lithuanian Prisoners

HOLY COMMUNION

When my soul sheds its tears,
when my heart languishes in longing,
when my whole being shivers in fatigue,
come, O Jesus, I beg You to come.
Draw near, Reviver and Consoler!
What is it You wish to tell me

by means of these people,
by these circumstances,
by this span of time?
Jesus, I implore You to shorten
the time of trial for us
for my dear ones, for my exhausted nation.
Jesus, I ask You – help those
who laid down their lives for our welfare;
assist them for whom You wish me to pray.

Lithuanian Prisoners

FOR THE HALLOWING OF SUFFERING

O Lord we pray thee for all weighed down with the mystery of suffering. Reveal thyself to them as the God of love who thyself doest bear all sufferings. Grant that they may know that suffering borne in fellowship with thee is not waste or frustration, but can be turned to goodness and blessing greater than if they had never suffered, through him who on the cross suffered rejection and hatred, loneliness and despair, agonizing pain and physical death, and rose victorious from the dead, conquering and to conquer, even Jesus Christ, our Lord.

George Appleton

––––––

What a vast ocean of human suffering is represented by the whole of the suffering on earth at any moment! But what makes up that mass? Blackness, deficiency, waste? No, we repeat, but rather potential energy. In suffering is concealed, with extreme intensity, the world's power of ascension. The whole problem is to liberate it by making it conscious of what it means and what it can achieve. What a leap forward the world would make towards God if all sick people at the same time converted their pain into a common desire that the reign of God should rapidly mature through the conquest and organization of the earth.

The Cross is the symbol and the focus of an action whose intensity is inexpressible. Even from an earthly

point of view, fully understood, Jesus crucified is not out-
cast or defeated. He is, on the contrary, the one who
bears the weight and bears always higher towards God the
progress of the universal advance. Let us do likewise, that
we may be united with him all the days of our life.

Teilhard de Chardin

FOR THE SICK IN MIND

O Holy Spirit who dost delve into all things, even the deep
things of God and the deep things of man, we pray thee
to penetrate the springs of personality of all who are sick
in mind, to bring them cleansing, healing and unity. Sanc-
tify all memory, dispel all fear, bring them to love thee
with all their mind and will, that they may be made whole
and glorify thee for ever.

George Appleton

A SUFFICIENT PRAYER

Lord, he whom thou lovest is sick. Do for him according
to his need, dear Lord.

George Appleton

———

There is only one way in which, with the world as it is,
God can show himself good in respect of man's suffering;
and that is by not asking of us anything that he is not
prepared to endure himself. He must share the dirt and
the sweat, the bafflement and loneliness, the pain, the
weakness, yes, and the death too. That would be a God
one could respect, a God who put aside all his magic
weapons, and did it all as one of us. A God who, when
we cry out in our misery (as we all do), 'Why should this
happen to me?' can answer truthfully, 'It happened to me

too, not because I couldn't help it happening, but because I chose that it should, because it was right'. Then and then alone will our doubts be stilled, not because we understand, but because we can trust.

John Austin Baker

As he crashes, the airman meets Christ and sees the pattern of salvation.

AIRMAN (*at the foot of the steps*)

Sir, I understand now what I ought to do.
Am I too late to bring to the wood of Your Cross
Whatever in me is guilty and ought to be crucified?
Whatever, being innocent, is privileged to die in Your
    Death?

PERSONA DEI

The moment when you meet Me is never too late,
Though the moment of death and the moment of choice
    were one.
Take up the Cross and come and follow Me,
For you shall carry the burden of bewilderment:
We shall find one another in the darkest hour of all.

Dorothy L. Sayers

I, if I be lifted up from the earth, will draw all men to me.

John 12: 32

If I can now forgive, it is only because I have been forgiven, I and all the other men and women who have ever lived. Certainly one can forgive only what has been done to oneself. But all the evil ever done has been done to God, because it is a misuse of his good gifts, a rejection of the purposes he set in motion from the beginning. The crucified Jesus is the only accurate picture of God the world has ever seen, and the hands that hold us in existence are pierced with unimaginable nails. But on this cross God fulfils the nature of forgiveness by using the evil done to him as the means to a new good; for it is the Cross of Jesus which creates within me a free, unhesitating acceptance of the law of love.

John Austin Baker

Nails would not have held God-and-Man fastened to the Cross, had Love not held Him there.

St Catherine of Siena

Wouldst thou learn thy Lord's meaning in this thing? Learn it well: Love was his meaning. Who showed it thee? Love. What showed He thee? Love. Wherefore showed it He? For Love.

Julian of Norwich

Once, in St Paul's Cathedral, I was listening to the magnificent chanting of the Nicene Creed. The setting reiterated and lingered over that one clause, 'He suffered'. 'He suffered, He suffered . . .' it was as if the singers could not get themselves away from the possessing word. They were but preluding the song of Heaven. The Lord, whom we shall worship, and rejoice in, and serve for ever – He is for ever He who suffered, and suffered so that to have suffered abides in Him in power through all the endless age.

H. C. G. Moule

ASCENSION PRAYER

Jesus, You revealed to us
an infinite secret of the soul:

31

mercy without limit, all-conquering love,
the power that springs from humility,
suffering, and sorrow;
all this You have manifested
as a healing balm for the soul.
Jesus, led by angels, Seraphim and Cherubim,
You ascended to heaven
for the jubilation of saints.

Lithuanian Prisoners

O Lord God, our heavenly Father, regard we beseech thee,
with thy divine pity the pains of all thy children; and grant
that the Passion of our Lord and his infinite love may
make fruitful for good the tribulations of the innocent, the
sufferings of the sick, and the sorrows of the bereaved;
through him who suffered in our flesh and died for our
sake, the same thy Son our Saviour Jesus Christ.

A prayer of the First World War, France 1915
Scottish Prayer Book 1929

CHRISTMAS VENITE

Let not my humble presence affront and stumble
your hardened hearts that have not known my ways
nor seen my tracks converge to this uniqueness.
Mine is the strength of the hills that endure and crumble,
bleeding slow fertile dust to the valley floor.
I am the fire in the leaf that crisps and falls
and rots into the roots of the rioting trees.
I am the mystery rising, surfacing
out of the seas into these infant eyes
that offer openness only and the unfocusing
search for an answering gaze. O recognize,
I am the undefeated heart of weakness.
Kneel to adore, fall down to pour your praise:
you cannot lie so low as I have been always.

John V. Taylor

'When He was born a man', she said, 'He put on the leaden shroud that's man's dying body. And on the Cross it bore Him down, sore heavy, dragging against the great nails, muffling God, blinding Him to the blindness of a man. But there, darkened within that shroud of mortal lead, beyond the furthest edge of hope, God had courage to trust yet in hopeless, helpless things, in gentle mercy, holiness, love crucified.

'And that courage, Wat, it was too rare and keen and quick a thing for sullen lead to prison, but instead it broke through, thinning lead, fining it to purest shining glass, to be a lamp for God to burn in.

'So men may have courage, then they will see how bright God shines.'

H. F. M. Prescott

4

DYING

The centre of this longer section consists of eight poems by one patient, Sidney Reeman. Accustomed to expressing his feelings in poetry, he kept writing throughout his stay of many weeks in St Christopher's. This selection charts something of his progress in thought and faith during that time. He speaks for many of the less articulate. Apart from contributions from two other patients, the rest of this collection of poetry and prose has been gathered during over 40 years of watching beside people as they draw near to death. They have all spoken to me at different times and still do.

Stevie Smith, D. H. Lawrence and John Bunyan need no introduction and most of the others I have included speak for themselves. Carlo Carretto's presentation of the spirit of St Francis brought out a deep response when read at our hospice prayers, as did several of my other choices. They, too, have stood the test of time.

Teilhard de Chardin's required point of submission leads on for me to two short poems composed for our poetry workshop where questions lead on to a final letting go. It is a letting go into the safety of God's hands, as John Austin Baker writes in this extract from *The Foolishness of God*, and of new life and love rising within us, as Brenda Dawson and others see it.

As I re-read this section I am left with a sense of a quiet security. Death can be a frightening mystery but we have seen so many who have gone trusting that a home awaits them. The help has often come through silence rather than from any words. Yet it is from words such as this collection that may come the ability to wait quietly, assured of the presence of a Grace far beyond anything we can offer.

STUDY TO DESERVE DEATH

Study to deserve Death, they only may
  Who fought well upon their earthly day,
Who never sheathed their swords or ran away.

See, such a man as this now proudly stands,
  Pale in the clasp of Death, and to his hands
Yields up the sword, but keeps the laurel bands.

Honour and emulate his warrior soul,
For whom the sonorous death-bells toll;
  He after journeying has reached his goal.

Prate not to me of suicide,
  Faint heart in battle, not for pride
I say Endure, but that such end denied
Makes welcomer yet the death that's to be died.

Stevie Smith

BEAUTIFUL OLD AGE

It ought to be lovely to be old
  to be full of the peace that comes of experience
and wrinkled ripe fulfilment.

The wrinkled smile of completeness that follows a life
  lived undaunted and unsoured with accepted lies.
If people lived without accepting lies
they would ripen like apples, and be scented like pippins
  in their old age.

Soothing, old people should be, like apples
  when one is tired of love.
Fragrant like yellowing leaves, and dim with the soft
  stillness and satisfaction of autumn.

And a girl should say:
  It must be wonderful to live and grow old.
Look at my mother, how rich and still she is!

And a young man should think: By Jove
  my father has faced all weathers, but it's been a life!

D. H. Lawrence

They then addressed themselves to the water, and entering, Christian began to sink, and, crying out to his good friend Hopeful, he said, I sink in deep waters; the billows go over my head, all His waves go over me. Selah.

Then said the other, Be of good cheer, my brother: I feel the bottom, and it is good. Then said Christian, Ah! my friend, the sorrows of death hath compassed me about, I shall not see the land that flows with milk and honey. And with that a great darkness and horror fell upon Christian, so that he could not see before him. Also here he in great measure lost his senses, so that he could neither remember nor orderly talk of any of those sweet refreshments that he had met with in the way of his pilgrimage.

[But Hopeful said], These troubles and distresses that you go through in these waters, are no sign that God hath forsaken you; but are sent to try you, whether you will call to mind that which heretofore you have received of His Goodness, and live upon Him in your distress.

Then I saw in my dream, that Christian was in a muse awhile. To whom also Hopeful added these words, Be of good cheer, Jesus Christ maketh thee whole. And with that Christian brake out with a loud voice, Oh, I see Him again; and He tells me, When thou passest through the waters, I will be with thee; and through the rivers, they shall not overflow thee. Then they both took courage, and the enemy was after that as still as a stone, until they were gone over. Christian therefore presently found ground to stand upon, and so it followed that the rest of the river was but shallow. Thus they got over.

John Bunyan

I think a lot of old people just aren't very sensible. They only have old friends and then they live to be ninety or something, like me, and then they start moaning because their friends have gone before, as they say.

My advice to the aged woman is find some young people. Don't go to these dreadful old folks' clubs but find some young people. Put up with their casualness because it's worth it. Why, I should like to know, are they so casual, I wonder?

I don't dread dying in my sleep but I do dread dying any other way. Mostly for the nuisance, you know. And I don't dread being dead. My heavenly Father has looked after me from the cradle and he won't stop at the grave. Through all my life he has taken care of me. Even if I just went out like a candle, what is there to dread?

Clergyman's widow, aged 92

DIMINUENDO

Age is a long, long weaning from the world.
I should have said that hardly yet had I the loving of it
   right.
Why learn to love and turn to go? Why sleep by day and
   night?
Now there is too much world to love, and no out that I
   know
But love more slow, but choose and go, but sleep by
   night and day
And only to unusual joy, rise up, rise up, obey.

Grace Goldin

———

'There need be no twilight. A man has Christ. Is he not the truth?' he whispered. 'Is he not the light? Is he not the keeper of the treasure we seek so blindly?'

An Islesman

We are dying, we are dying, so all we can do
is now to be willing to die and build the ship
of death to carry the soul on the longest journey.

A little ship, with oars and food
and little dishes, and all accoutrements
fitting and ready for the departing soul.

37

Now launch the small ship, now as the body dies
and life departs, launch out, the fragile soul
in the fragile ship of courage, the ark of faith
with its store of food and little cooking pans
and change of clothes,
upon the flood's black waste
upon the waters of the end.

D. H. Lawrence

What is death?
Every day I tell myself: Death is like
someone who has risen from a grave illness.
Every day I tell myself: Death is like breathing
a fragrance, like being in an intoxicating land.
Every day I tell myself: Death is like the
moment when the heavens clear for an
instant and a man goes out with his net
to catch birds, and suddenly finds himself
in an unknown place!

What is death?
It is an upright heart, when her time has come.

Ancient Egyptian song

Life and death were but two aspects of one and the same thing, as also sorrow and joy, light and darkness, cold and heat.

It was as though the real were cut in half by a door.

With good reason had Christ chosen the image: 'I am the door.'

The door is the same on both sides.

The earth, the visible, the tangible, time and space, are on this side; heaven, the invisible, the eternal, the infinite, are on the other side.

But everything is one, congruent, logical and true.

The door which is Christ simultaneously rules the here and the beyond with his love, crucified on this side, glorified on the other.

To become immortal and enter the glory of the Risen Christ, everyone must pass through this door, and the One who opens and closes it is the Lord. As Revelation says, 'If I open, no one closes.'

And creatures, through him, have two aspects: one crucified, here, and one glorious, beyond.

Nobody can escape this fact, and hence the death of each individual has a sorrowful aspect in the here-now and a glorious aspect in hope.

Our passing is always a fearsome ordeal, like looking at a boundless sea – and then, the explosion of joy as you watch the sea part!

So it was for the People of God, and so it is for us.

There is always the painful wait, then a sudden light.

The wait is yours, the light is God's.

And it is free.

You can never claim you have deserved it.

On the contrary!

No merit has the power to open the door.

Only God's love freely given can manage this impassable lock.

'When he closes, nobody can open' (Revelation 3: 7).

But his will is always prompt to open for 'This is why I came into the world, so that they can have life and have it to the full' (John 10: 10).

How often have you asked, 'Why am I still here?'

And the reply is always the same.

You must learn to love. For beyond the door there is nothing – except love.

Carlo Carretto

Soon we shall die and all memory of those people will have left the earth, and we ourselves shall be loved for a while and forgotten. But the love will have been enough; all those impulses of love return to the love that made them. Even memory is not necessary for love. There is a land of the living and a land of the dead, and the bridge is love, the only survival, the only meaning.

The last words of Thornton Wilder's novel,
The Bridge of San Luis Rey

After a life of many vicissitudes and some months of pain, Sidney Reeman was found to have cancer of his gullet, already inoperable. During his four months in St Christopher's Hospice he found peace and started writing poetry again after a long gap.

From a series of poems written before his death.

BUTTERFLIES

Lord, it would be idle
to pretend that I have no fears;
Even tho' I am full of faith
And I am mindful of thy mercy,
And I am hedged about
By your almighty assurances,
I still advance towards you
With joy in anticipation
And fear of the uncharted seas,
Although I know not the day
Of your beckoning, my faith tells me
To mark off the days like a homesick
Schoolboy puts pen through the days
Separating him from homecoming,
So I, above all, long for the freedom
Of the sons of God. Lord give me
Inward peace, take away all fear.

Sidney G. Reeman
19 Jan. 1975

PRESSING BUSINESS

As life gathers momentum
And one reaches
The Tattenham Corner of the soul
The galloping hooves are thudding
As one races for the post
Lord, so little time and so much to do
Love urges us on
You have given me peace and happiness

In which to end my days
There is so much to do
Sweeping and cleaning
To make room for You
Such a sense of urgency
To commit thoughts to paper
So little time and so much to do
Lord, urge me on.

Sidney G. Reeman
23 Jan. 1975

INCOME AND EXPENDITURE

It costs much
To give ourselves
It costs much more
To be the recipient
This requires humility
No man likes to lose
His measure of independence
Suddenly the ground has given way
From under his feet.
Our resources are like a rivulet
Which has drained dry
And we have to ask for water
But I know I depend on Christ
And so it is to Him I turn
The Fountain of Living Water
I shall not thirst,
I am not too proud
To beg of the Lord,
Thanks be to God.

Sidney G. Reeman
25 Jan. 1975

IN THE MIDST OF LIFE

Death and I are only nodding acquaintances
We have not been formally introduced
But many times I have noticed
The final encounter
Here in this hospice,
I can truly say
That death has been met with dignity
Who can divine the thoughts
Of a man in close confrontation?
I can only remember
One particular passing
When a man,
With sustained smile
Pointed out what was for him
Evidently a great light
Who knows what final revelations
Are received in the last hours?
Lord, grant me a star in the East
As well as a smouldering sunset.

Sidney G. Reeman
28 Jan. 1975

MURMURINGS

Low murmurings from your creation, Lord
Despite the fact that I am full of thy praise.
In your supreme wisdom, Lord,
You have endowed me
With something more than I can swallow.
I do not pretend to understand
The pattern of your handiwork
Save that in a mysterious way
It helps me to magnify you.
You have wrought wonders in me, Lord,
No slim volume would suffice
To contain the Litany of your praise.
But perhaps a booklet
For, dare I call them, bones of contention,

For example, in the midst of tribulation
Was it quite necessary, Lord,
To allow my specs to nose-dive
And break on the bathroom floor?

Sidney G. Reeman
3 Feb. 1975

COMING UP FOR THE THIRD TIME

Lord, in the last six days,
I have felt peculiarly plaintive,
Strength seems to be ebbing away
My tale is a tale of woe
Now in the midst of a melancholy moment
Preoccupation about pain
And thoughts squandered about swallowing
I realise that I am
A man of little faith
And it is certainly true
That if Christ were to beckon me
Across the waves, immediately
I should begin to sink
Through sheer lack of confidence
Lord, confirm me in faith
Each time you come with comfort
As the Bread of Life, then
I shall realise that the Divine Strength
Is not ebbing away,
But gathering in intensity.

Sidney G. Reeman
7 Feb. 1975

HEAVEN

The imagination runs riot
In visualising heaven.
Is heaven really
Like the background music

To a Hollywood biblical epic?
Is heaven a magnified
Hallelujah Chorus
Sung by an augmented
Huddersfield Choir?
We can easily imagine
What heaven is not.
All I need to know
This side of the trumpets sounding
Is that heaven
Is the vision of my God
Seeing all things and acting in Him.

Sidney G. Reeman
9 Feb. 1975

LOST PROPERTY

Priceless is that which I have lost
Priceless because irretrievable.
Two days at least seemed
To have passed me by
In a fortnight of existence
Rather uncanny
To think that yesterday is today
And today is yesterday
But the hospice has given reassurance
As well as sustenance
Has given me twelve large hampers
Duly strained and liquidised
The Bread of Life here below
The Great Supper is awaiting
Ever awaiting.

Sidney G. Reeman
24 Feb. 1975

Sidney died in the morning of 1 March 1975.

I am standing on the sea shore. A ship sails and spreads her white sails to the morning breeze and starts for the ocean. She is an object of beauty and I stand watching her till at last she fades on the horizon and someone at my side says, 'She is gone.' Gone where? Gone from my sight, that is all; she is just as large in the masts, hull and spars as she was when I saw her, and just as able to bear her load of living freight to its destination.

The diminished size and total loss of sight is in me, not in her; and just at the moment when someone at my side says, 'She is gone', there are others who are watching her coming, and other voices take up a glad shout, 'There she comes', and that is Dying.

Source unknown

———

The mountain tarn empties itself by evaporation; its waters are stolen away by sunbeams; they have not perished, they have given themselves to the sunbeams; and have suffered change, and now in the subtle, impalpable form of mist they can steal up the hot bare crags of the mountain and invade with freshness its most secret glens, and soon, when the air grows cool, will hang jewels upon every gossamer thread and bring life to every fainting leaf and blade of grass. So Christ by His sacrifice for us, by the self-emptying of the Incarnation, acquired a new power of stealing into wounded and sorrowful hearts in their extremest dejection and dryness. He comes by His saving death to dying people . . . The mystery of Christ's love in death can steal into that silence, and fill that supreme emptiness . . . In the hour of death and the day of judgement, Good Lord, deliver us.

Fr Congreve

You were my death;
You I could hold
when all fell away from me.

Paul Celan
Forms of Prayer for Jewish Worship

Thou angel of God who hast charge of me,
From the dear Father of mercifulness
The shepherding kind of the folds of the saints mighty
To make round about me this night:

Drive from me every temptation and danger,
Surround me on the sea of unrighteousness,
And in the narrows, crooks and straits
Keep thou my coracle, keep it always.

Be thou a bright flame before me,
Be thou a guiding star above me,
Be thou a smooth path below me,
And be a kindly shepherd behind me,
Today, Tonight and for ever.

I am tired and I am a stranger,
Lead thou me to the land of angels;
For me it is time to go home
To the court of Christ, to the place of Heaven.

We have come a long way, Christianly speaking, from the
justly criticised notion of 'submission to the will of God'
which is in danger of weakening and softening the fine
steel of the human will, brandished against all the powers
of darkness and diminishment ... I can only unite myself
to the will of God (as endured passively) when all my
strength is spent ... Unless I do everything I can to
advance or resist, I shall not find myself at the required
point – I shall not submit to God as much as I might have
done or as much as He wishes. If on the contrary, I per-

severe courageously, I shall rejoin God across evil, deeper down than evil; I shall draw close to Him.

Teilhard de Chardin

The poems printed below were written by a patient who spent seven months with us; she was almost blind and could not use her hands. She was adamant that she could not produce poems; however, after attending the workshop she eventually wrote several, dictating them.

'Off the Cuff' was composed only a few days before she died.

STARTING POINT

Where do we begin?
    At the starting point 'X'
And 'X' is also the unknown quantity
    Through 'X' we find 'Y'
'X' + 'Y' leaves us also questioning.
What are we questioning?
    What are we seeking?
I always seem to be looking for something –
    Even in dreams I am searching
For something – I am not sure what.
    Just as I seem to get there
Another door opens and the scene changes
    And I keep on walking and walking
Until the scene fades and I wake up
    The equation still unsolved.

Margaret Drake

OFF THE CUFF

Quite suddenly, off the cuff, it came to me,
'Midst our laughing, chattering, joking and repartee,
The cheery 'See yer!' 'Take care!' and 'Goodbyee!',
A sudden silence, slow unwinding,
    blessed peace and solitude.

Margaret Drake

Thine eyes shall see the king in his beauty: they shall behold the land that is very far off.

Isaiah 33: 17

NOTHING TO SAVE

There is nothing to save, now all is lost,
but a tiny core of stillness in the heart
like the eye of a violet.

D. H. Lawrence

———

I rest on God, who will assuredly not allow me to find the meaning of life in his love and forgiveness, to be wholly dependent upon him for the gift of myself, and then destroy that meaning, revoke that gift. He who holds me in existence now, can and will hold me in it still, through and beyond the dissolution of my mortal frame. For this is the essence of love, to affirm the right of the beloved to exist. And what God affirms, nothing and no one can contradict.

John Austin Baker

THE GATE OF THE YEAR

I said to the man who stood at the Gate of the Year –
  'Give me a light that I may tread safely into the unknown.'
  And he replied:
  'Go out into the darkness and put your hand into the hand of God. That shall be to you better than light and safer than a known way.'

Minnie Haskins

———

If I should die and leave you here awhile,
Be not like others – sore undone, who keep
Long vigils by the silent dust and weep.

For my sake turn again to life and smile,
    Nerving thy heart and trembling hands to do
Something to comfort weaker hearts than thine.
    Complete those dear unfinished tasks of mine
And I perchance may therein comfort you.

Anon

I have seen death too often to believe in death.
    It is not an ending, but a withdrawal.
As one who finishes a long journey
    Stills the motor, turns off the lights,
Steps from his car
    And walks up the path to the home that awaits him.

An American poet

To the hands that broke and gave life to the bread that
blessed and caressed, that were pierced . . . to the kindly
and mighty hands that reach down to the very marrow of
the soul – that mould and create – to the hands through
which so great a love is transmitted – it is to these hands
that it is good to surrender our soul . . .

Source unknown

THROUGH A GLASS DARKLY

It's lucky our eyes look outward
We can't see how we look
Without mirrors.
As our bodies diminish
Or lose their shape
It's the others who see it.
We feel its limitations.
How do we look in their eyes?
Does it hurt our family and friends
To see us changed so much?
As we move lifewards

49

So we become transformed.
Through our dark internal glass we see clearly
But the eyes of our friends cloud over.
In their concern they recall us
As we used to be, loving and alive
But they seem unable to see the new life
Rising within us.

Brenda Dawson,
28 June 1986

Oh! think of stepping ashore,
And finding it heaven;
To clasp a hand outstretched,
And to find it God's hand!
To breathe new air
And find that celestial air;
To feel refreshed,
And find it immortality;
Oh! think to step from storm and stress
To one unbroken calm:
To awake and find it home.

Anon

In death we meet the conqueror of death; we meet love.

F. M. M. Comper

5

GONE AWAY

The first days after a bereavement are often numb and almost devoid of feeling. The assurance that all is well with the one who is lost may surmount the pain that has hardly begun. I have therefore made a rather arbitrary division between this and the next section, looking quietly for a moment at the early comfort that the end of the weakness and suffering that may accompany dying can bring. The words 'Rest eternal' were indeed well chosen centuries ago.

The thoughts of a home of peace and reunion are given in the words of earth, but we have no other words to use for what we think of in faith. Once again, and perhaps surprising to some, we find words from Jewish prayer books. George Appleton links the unknown world with ours in his meditation on the 'Go-between Lord' while Boros gives the link between us yet another dimension.

Gerard Manley Hopkins' beautiful poem presents the assurance of the all-embracing concern of Christ. Out of sight is never out of the mind of God. The two poems translated so beautifully by Helen Waddell come from centuries ago as does the comforting phrase from the Syrian saint. We are fellow citizens with them as we are with those we have lost ourselves. The poem of salute to the Abbot of the Dark Ages that ends the section may have been written while he was still alive but in those times earthly parting must so often have been for ever. The phrases 'City safe for my bewildered heart' and 'Love's own singing follows' have echoed in my mind for many years.

Peace shall come in the day which is known unto the Lord,
and it shall be neither day nor night such as now is, but

everlasting light, infinite brightness, steadfast peace and secure rest.

Thomas à Kempis, The Imitation of Christ

After long years alone,
Ironed to flesh and bone,
It is most sweet to pass
Like wind above the grass,
Free ever, and to find
The waiting mind.

Then to set forth together,
To know the new strange weather,
And where the new road leads;
To put old burdens by,
And have the wind and sky,
Light as the wild-duck's feather
Or dandelion seeds.

John Masefield

PRAYER IN THE HOME BEFORE A FUNERAL

Merciful Father, be with us as we gather in this house, the home of our dear one who has gone forward to life everlasting. We remember all her goodness. May her memory be a blessing.

Help us to remember that the soul does not die, and our dear one has gone to that eternal home which You prepared for us when our work on earth is done, and our time here has ended. Open the gates of mercy for her. May she enter into everlasting peace. In Your light we see beyond the frontiers of death to the life that has no end.

This house was built by human hands, but we shall come together in a home where we shall never part, surrounded by Your presence.   Amen.

Forms of Prayer for Jewish Worship

The gates of heaven mayest thou find opened,
And the tower of peace mayest thou see,
And the dwellings of confidence,
And angels of peace to meet thee with joy,
And may the High Priest stand to receive thee;
And thou,
Go thou to the end,
For thou shalt rest,
And rise up again . . .

The gates of the sanctuary may Michael open,
And bring the soul as an offering before God;
And may the redeeming angel accompany thee
Unto the gates of the Heavens, where Israel dwells;
May it be vouchsafed to thee
To stand in this beautiful place;
And thou,
Go thou to the end,
For thou shalt rest,
And rise up again.

Jewish Prayer, *Sephardi Prayer Book*

St Luke wrote the story of the child who died even as Jesus was on the way to her home with her parents. She was healed after all. The one we loved was not. Can we still reach them? Is our grieving only self-pity? Or is that love, which seems to reach out with nowhere to go, still a way of linking us together and of somehow bringing our power of loving back into this world?

NO TROUBLE TO HIM
Luke 8: 49

Your daughter is dead; do not trouble the Master
any more.

There is nothing more to be done,
nothing that anyone can do
except to bury the dead.

An hour earlier
　　　it might have been of some use,
　　　but now it is too late,
　　　don't bother the Master.

The Master's reply –
　　　Do not fear, only believe
　　　all shall be well;
　　　there is no death,
　　　only sleep.
　　　falling asleep here – waking there,
　　　still within reach of the Master's voice.

The Master spans both worlds,
　　　this and that,
　　　can hear the messages we send
　　　and speak them on the other side,
　　　take the love of our hearts
　　　and warm theirs.

To each one who crosses the border
　　　He says
　　　Little one, rise
　　　Faith restores each little one to her parents.

So trouble the Master –
　　　trust in His over-arching care
　　　radio-ing messages of love
　　　through Him.

Don't neglect the gift
　　　of a go-between Lord;
　　　don't fail those ahead
　　　by neglectful forgetfulness.

She is not dead, she slept
　　　and woke, and still
　　　is within the sound of His voice.

It is no trouble to the Master
　　　for He, too, has slept that sleep
　　　and awakened.

George Appleton

The death of someone we love can become a gift and a grace for us despite the pain that fills the foreground. That person is, of course, already safe in God's mercy. But we have 'buried' the memory of him into our life. As Rilke said: 'As regards myself, what died, died into my own heart.' In other words, we think of the good and fine things the dead person did in his life, and of the possibilities that are still open to him, thus repeatedly rendering him present in our life, drawing on the beauty of a life that is already united with God. We are completing his earthly life for him and sharing in a destiny united to God. Perhaps people will one day think of us in this way.

In order to make clear to some degree the presence of the dead and their power to help, we have to start with quite simple everyday, matter-of-fact experiences. An example would be that of the remoteness of someone actually present and of the presence of someone far away. Persons may be in the room with us, so close that we could touch them. We see them, talk to them, ask questions which they answer, and they ask us questions. They are there. And yet perhaps we feel that, despite all our various points of contact, they are not really present; they do not really mean anything to us.

We may have the contrary experience. Someone else, a friend or other person dear to us who is on the other side of the globe, or already dead, is essentially closer to us than the human being who is in our room. It is one of the principal (but frequently neglected) functions of philosophy to reflect on such everyday experience.

The very nature of love involves a statement that is made whenever and wherever love is felt: 'For you I exist, I am there.' This includes another statement, not so clear but no less real: 'It is so true that I exist for you and in your eyes, that you cannot die, cannot wholly disappear from my presence.'

The light shed on this world by the beloved dead gives the living a glimpse of the glory of a world to come; he becomes aware of his own hope, feels the closeness of God whose mercy and love surrounds the departed forever.

Ladislaus Boros

THE LANTERN OUT OF DOORS

Sometimes a lantern moves along the night.
That interests our eyes. And who goes there?
I think; where from and bound, I wonder, where,
With, all down darkness wide, his wading light?

Men go by me whom either beauty bright
In mould or mind or what not else makes rare:
They rain against our much-thick and marsh air
Rich beams, till death or distance buys them quite.

Death or distance soon consumes them: wind
What most I may eye after, be in at the end
I cannot, and out of sight is out of mind.

Christ minds: Christ's interest, what to avow or amend
There, eyes them, heart wants, care haunts, foot follows
   kind,
Their ransom, their rescue, and first, fast, last friend.

Gerard Manley Hopkins

———

Those who die in grace are no further from us than God
and God is very near.

4th century Syrian saint

The
souls of the just
are in the hands of God.
They that trust in him
shall understand the truth
and they that are faithful in love
shall rest in him.

Wisdom 3: 9

Thou hast come safe to port
I still at sea,
The light is on thy head,
Darkness in me.

Pluck thou in heaven's field
Violet and rose,
While I strew flowers that will thy vigil keep
Where thou dost sleep,
Love, in thy last repose.

translated by Helen Waddell

And he came and preached peace to you who were far off
and peace to those who were near, for through him we
both have access in one Spirit to the Father. So then you
are no more strangers and sojourners, but you are fellow
citizens with the saints and members of the household of
God.

Ephesians 2: 17–19

STILL IN THY HAND

O God, Creator and Father of all; we know that those
whom we love and who have died are still in thy hand in
the world of spirit. Grant them, O Lord, courage and grace
that they may grow into that likeness which is thy will for
them. And when we die, grant that our loved ones may
be there to welcome us to that spiritual country which is
our true home, through Jesus Christ our Lord.

George Appleton

O Lord, we pray for those throughout the world who die
for what they believe to be the right and when they have
passed to the light eternal, show them thy truth.

Anon

With Jesus to find restfulness
In the blest habitation of peace,
In the paradise of gentleness,
In the fairy-bower of release
    Mercy-arrayed

Traditional Gaelic

TO GRIMOLD, ABBOT OF ST GALL

Then live, my strength, anchor of weary ships,
    Safe shore and land at last, thou, for my wreck,
My honour, thou, and my abiding rest,
    My city safe for a bewildered heart.
What though the plains and mountains and the sea
    Between us are, that which no earth can hold
Still follows thee, and loves own singing follows,
    Longing that all things may be well with thee.
Christ who first gave thee for a friend to me,
Christ keep thee well, where'er thou art, for me.
    Earth's self shall go and the swift wheel of heaven
Perish and pass, before our love shall cease.
    Do but remember me, as I do thee,
And God, who brought us on this earth together,
    Bring us together in His house of heaven.

Hrabanus Maurus,
translated by Helen Waddell

6

LEFT BEHIND

Mourning, being left behind, is painful and long and dangerous, as Margery Allingham says in my choice for a beginning to this section. But as she says 'the end is gain' and I have tried here to put together prose and poetry that speak of ways along this difficult journey. The very stores of memory which hurt so much at the beginning gradually give the help and strength to go on. Again, I turn to Kushner, Frankl and Jewish prayers and then to Nora Leney, whose daughter died with us some years ago, and her two poignant poems. A moment of unexpected joy suddenly comes across her desolation to bring peace.

Christus Consolator was written by Bishop Handley Moule early in the First World War and I found in it a dependable comfort to which I turned again and again. It was my constant first choice to hold on to in the often muddled feelings of a bereavement.

Father Bede Jarrett's prayer appears to be the source of the title to the book, although it was only after discussion with my original editor in a different context that I realized how apt it was for what I was trying to share.

Old and new guilts and angers can be so powerful and disturbing that it is often difficult to see these in perspective as an almost inevitable part of normal grieving. They can make it very hard to recognize and use the opportunity for growth that lies in the heart of loss. That it should be a growing point, as Harvey calls it, seems almost a betrayal at first. Later, the appearance of courage and new commitment can make one feel as hypocritical as Bonhoeffer when he writes from prison. Slowly, one learns afresh who one is and that there can be new duties and fulfilments.

Many of Henry Vaughan's poems were written from bereavement. The one here which I chose to learn by heart promises light for the journey, that those we have lost are 'that Cities shining spires we travell to'. They lead us on to new faith, and a second sowing. 'Grief is not for ever — but love is' and the heart that has been enlarged by the experience has something strong to pass on.

Mourning is not forgetting. It is an undoing. Every minute tie has to be untied and something permanent and valuable recovered and assimilated from the knot. The end is gain, of course. Blessed are they that mourn, for they shall be made strong, in fact. But the process is like all other human births, painful and long and dangerous.

Margery Allingham

LI FU-JEN

The sound of her silk skirt has stopped.
On the marble pavement dust grows.
Her empty room is cold and still.
Fallen leaves are piled against the doors.
   Longing for that lovely lady
How can I bring my aching heart to rest.

translated by Arthur Waley

———

I cannot ask for power to forget, but I can ask for greater courage to remember.

Source unknown

They have healed the wound of my people lightly, saying 'Peace, peace', when there is no peace.

Jeremiah 6: 4

FINALE

A tree left haggard
　　By lightning's scorching strike;
He sits with fixed unfocused stare
　　Too dry to weep. Almost life seems
Extinct in his still form, yet secretly
　　A gentler flame is kindling
Memory's eager fuel, and soon
　　Moments of remembered love will start
To spread their healing power
　　Through his hurt spirit.

B. M. W. Trapnell

Where do you get the strength to go on, when you have used up all of your own strength? Where do you turn for patience when you have run out of patience, when you have been more patient for more years than anyone should be asked to be, and the end is nowhere in sight? I believe that God gives us strength and patience and hope, renewing our spiritual resources when they run dry. How else do sick people manage to find more strength and more good humour over the course of prolonged illness than any one person could possibly have, unless God was constantly replenishing their souls? How else do widows find the courage to pick up the pieces of their lives and go out to face the world alone, when, on the day of their husband's funeral, they did not have that courage? How else do the parents of a retarded or brain-damaged youngster wake up every morning and turn again to their responsibilities, unless they are able to lean on God when they grow weak?

We don't have to beg or bribe God to give us strength or hope or patience. We need only turn to Him, admit that we can't do this on our own, and understand that bravely bearing up under long-term illness is one of the most human, and one of the most godly, things we can ever do. One of the things that constantly reassures me that God is real, and not just an idea that religious leaders made up, is the fact that people who pray for strength, hope and courage so often find resources of strength, hope and courage that they did not have before they prayed.

Harold S. Kushner

Let us learn like a bird for a moment to take
Sweet rest on a branch that is ready to break – She feels
   the branch tremble,
Yet gaily she sings,
What is it to her?
She has wings, she has wings!

Anon

In the past, nothing is irrecoverably lost, but everything irrevocably stored ... having been is the surest kind of being.

Viktor Frankl

Two poems written by the mother of a girl who died when she was only 22 after two years in the hospice.

QUESTION

Two souls run parallel
   could it be?
One myself
   The other watching me?
Two souls suffering differently
One aches and weeps
The other takes it philosophically.

Strange feelings in affinity
   one knows that time will heal
the other wants to grieve,
   one carries burdens deep within that rend the
   heart to see
the other too tired to deceive.

So we struggle on
myself and I
I take it on the chin
and I just cry.

Nora Leney

Today a song-bird sang –
Perched so high on yonder tree
Against a sky of silver grey
Full throated song to fill the air
And lift.all care away –
I stayed to listen.

Nora Leney

You, O Lord, are the endless power that renews life beyond death; You are the greatness that saves. You care for the living with love. You renew life beyond death with unending mercy. You support the falling, and heal the sick. You free prisoners, and keep faith with those who sleep in the dust. Who can perform such mighty deeds, and who can compare with you, a king who brings death and life, and renews salvation. You are faithful to renew life beyond death. Blessed are You Lord, who renews life beyond death.

Forms of Prayer for Jewish Worship

But just now we are thinking not of the redeeming virtue of the crucified Lord. Rather, we are looking on Him as wonderfully fitted, by the 'unknown' sufferings of His sacrifice, to be *Christus Consolator*. We have thought about His heart, broken for our sakes, only that we may get into the living depths of the truth that He now is able, indeed able, 'to bind up the broken-hearted'.

To get thus at Him we have together climbed the steps of some subordinate reasons for hope and cheer, advancing all the while towards the sanctuary of peace at the top. And here on the quiet summit, we find, as we have seen already, not a truth merely but a Person. Strong in His personal love and willingness, rich with His unspeakably personal experience, He is able to 'be touched with the feeling of our infirmities' and our wounds. He is 'able to save, to the uttermost', from all their weariness and their heavy loads, those who will let Him have His way. He is able, with personal methods of His own, to transfigure sorrows into joys. Consider HIM. Let it sink always deeper into your torn and tired spirit that such a Person exists, that this Person exists – living, loving accessible. He is 'the Man at the Gate' whom readers of the *Pilgrim's Progress* will remember. 'Here is a poor burthened sinner', said the Pilgrim, 'I would know, Sir, if you are willing to let me in'. 'Here', let us say, 'are stricken and broken hearts; we have heard, Sir, that your heart was once broken, and has stood open ever since, and that its great rift is turned into a gate by which men go in and find peace. We would know if you are willing to let us in.'

'I am willing with all my heart', said the Man; and with that He opened the gate.

H. C. G. Moule

RICHARD RAINOLDES
Deceased 1 December 1582

One of the three bailiffs who welcomed Queen Elizabeth to Burford A.D. 1574. On his tomb is this word to his wife:

I go to sle	And Wee
epe befo	shal wake
re You	Togeather

We seem to give them back to thee, O God, who gavest them to us; yet, as thou dost not lose them in giving, so we do not lose them by their return.

Not as the world gives givest thou, O Lover of souls.

What thou givest thou takest not away; for what is thine is ours also if we are thine; and life is eternal and love is immortal; and death is only our horizon, and our horizon is nothing save the limits of our sight.

Lift us up, strong Son of God, that we may see further. Cleanse our eyes that we may see more clearly; draw us closer to thyself, that we may know ourselves to be nearer to our loved ones who are with thee. And while thou dost prepare a place for us, prepare us also for that happy place, that where thou art we may also be for evermore.

The prayer of Father Bede Jarrett O.P.
Syon Abbey, Devon

This is not meant to imply that no difficulties exist or arise, nor that everything in the garden is already lovely. My contention is that the death of a loved person is at root a growing-point, with all the pain and struggle which that phrase suggests. It is undeniable, and indeed central to this picture of death, that there is a self-exposure promoted by the tearing away of a prop. The distinction at stake is not between a painless separation and a painful one, but between bereavement seen as a genuinely critical, creative moment or phase in a person's development, and bereavement relegated to the less than human category of things to be got over. This latter way of picturing the matter suggests a salvage operation, a stoical return to 'normality', rather than a boundless opportunity, an opening up to God, to one's true self, to all that was and is and is to be.

Nicholas Peter Harvey

WHO AM I?

Who am I? They often tell me
I would step from my cell's confinement
calmly, cheerfully, firmly,
like a squire from his country-house.

Who am I? They often tell me
I would talk to my warders
freely and friendly and clearly,
as though it were mine to command.

Who am I? They also tell me
I would bear the days of misfortune
equably, smilingly, proudly,
like one accustomed to win.

Am I then really all that which other men tell of?
Or am I only what I myself know of myself?
restless and longing and sick, like a bird in a cage,
struggling for breath, as though hands were compressing
   my throat,
yearning for colours, for flowers, for the voices of birds,
thirsting for words of kindness, for neighbourliness,
trembling with anger at despotisms and petty
   humiliation,
tossing in expectation of great events,
powerlessly trembling for friends at an infinite distance
weary and empty at praying, at thinking, at making,
faint, and ready to say farewell to it all?

Who am I? This or the other?
Am I one person today and tomorrow another?
Am I both at once? A hypocrite before others,
and before myself a contemptibly woebegone weakling?
Or is something within me still like a beaten army,
fleeing in disorder from victory already achieved?

Who am I? They mock me, these lonely questions of
   mine.
Whoever I am, Thou knowest, O God, I am thine.

Dietrich Bonhoeffer

He who binds to himself a joy
Doth the wingèd life destroy;
But he who kisses the joy as it flies
Lives in Eternity's sun rise.

William Blake

All suffering has an end, David, if only you wait long
enough. Try to remember that. Sorrow has its life just like
people. Sorrow is born and lives and dies. And when it's
dead and gone, someone's left behind to remember it.
Exactly like people.

Anne Holm

Joy of my life! while left me here,
    And still my Love!
How in thy absence thou dost steere
    Me from above!
    A life well lead
    This truth commends.
    With quick, or dead
    It never ends.

Stars are of mighty use: The night
    Is dark, and long;
The Rode foul, and where one goes right,
    Six may go wrong.
    One twinkling ray
    Shot o'r some cloud
    May clear much way
    And guide a croud.

Gods Saints are shining lights: who stays
   Here long must passe
O're dark hills, swift streames, and steep ways
   As smooth as glasse;
   But these all night
   Like candles, shed
   Their beams, and light
   Us into Bed.

They are (indeed) our Pillar-fires
   Seen as we go,
They are that Cities shining spires
   We travell too;
   A swordlike gleame
   Kept man for sin
   First *Out*; This beame
   Will guide him *In*.

Henry Vaughan

In bereavement we all know that at first memories of happiness shared bring the tears more than almost anything else. A photograph of somewhere we spent that wonderful day, the flowers we planted together, the music we loved to listen to, all break our hearts. But after a time we can bear to think of these things, and it is good to remember how much happiness there was. Sometimes, indeed, it is only after the other has gone that we realise how much there was. At the time we used to fuss and grumble so, that we hardly noticed the deep inner contentment we shared with them. There is a lesson here: Remember the good things. Remember them as they happen day by day. Be grateful for them as they go by. Then later on they will be a strength and consolation. It is because we remember the 'pastures green' and the 'quiet waters' that we are aware of God's rod and staff comforting us even in the darkest valley.

John Austin Baker

The writer of this poem lost his wife in the hospice, he returned as a volunteer and later joined the poetry workshop.

SOLITUDE

The sun is setting
As I sit in my garden listening to the wonderful
   songs of the birds.
A gentle breeze is blowing
I seem to 'feel' the fragrant smell of the many mints
Eau-de-Cologne, peppermint, lemon mint,
I observe the lovely rosemary with its clusters of
   beautiful blue flowers
The humble cowslips and dandelions seem to shout
   We have beauty too.
Memories come to me of the Loved One who used to
   sit with me here.
I feel so thankful to the Dear Lord for this moment
   of so happy reunion.

How privileged I do feel to be here.
It is now time to leave.
Goodnight my loved one.
Goodnight sun.
Goodnight birds.
Goodnight lovely flowers.
I feel so happy, so relaxed.
God bless to one and all.

                                        Martin Lange

Bereavement is the deepest initiation into the mysteries of human life, an initiation more searching and profound than even happy love. Love remembered and consecrated by grief belongs more clearly than the happy intercourse of friends to the eternal world; it has proved itself stronger than death.

Bereavement is the sharpest challenge to our trust in God; if faith can overcome this there is no mountain which it cannot remove. And faith can overcome it. It brings the eternal world nearer to us and makes it seem more real.

                                        Dean Inge

SECOND SOWING

For whom
The milk ungiven in the breast
When the child is gone?

For whom
The love locked up in the heart
That is left alone?
That golden yield
Split sod once, overflowed an August field,
Threshed out in pain upon September's floor,
Now hoarded high in barns, a sterile store.

Break down the bolted door;
Rip open, spread and pour
The grain upon the barren ground
Wherever crack in clod is found.

There is no harvest for the heart alone;
The seed of love must be
Eternally
Resown.

Ann Morrow Lindbergh

Grief is not for ever – but love is.

Anon

7

RESURRECTION

There are times when a sudden lifting of the load of longing and pain comes across the path of bereavement. For a moment the loss is transformed into gain in an almost miraculous way. Resurrection seems the only appropriate word.

It seemed right to begin this section with John Bunyan, whose scriptural vision of the pilgrims' rise from the river of death into the joy of eternal life has comforted so many down the years. Much less well-known are the thoughts of Harry Williams, first presented in a Lent Book in 1951. The picture of all our fragmentary experiences of love and joy and peace and beauty gathered together for ever with nothing lost or left behind, I have found equally consoling and the whole booklet has constantly been referred to.

A further extract from Dorothy Sayers' *The Just Vengeance* with its list of transformations leads into the selections from favourite authors. The two George Herbert poems are beautifully set for solo and chorus by Vaughan Williams and I must be one of many who have burst joyfully into 'Rise heart, thy Lord is risen'. This truth is close to us through the spirit and rings through my other choices in this section.

John Taylor's prayer comes as a challenge to us all, even though we may feel we scarcely have the energy to respond. Grief is so very exhausting. So I end with Helen Waddell's translation of Alfred the Great's transcription of Boethius, a quieter look at the joy of a trustful acceptance. Our God is himself the end and the beginning and he goes before us to the journey's completion. Perhaps the mystery of all our little resurrections joined together in the light of the God who himself died and rose again can only truly be hinted at in poetry.

Christian and Hopeful have come through the river of death:

Now upon the bank of the river, on the other side, they saw the two shining men again, who there waited for them. Wherefore being come out of the river, they saluted them, saying, We are ministering spirits, sent forth to minister for those that shall be heirs of salvation. Thus they went along towards the gate.

Now you must note, that the City stood upon a mighty hill; but the pilgrims went up that hill with ease, because they had these two men to lead them up by the arms; also they had left their mortal garments behind them in the river; for though they went in with them, they came out without them. They therefore went up here with much agility and speed, though the foundation upon which the City was framed was higher than the clouds; they therefore went up through the regions of the air, sweetly talking as they went, being comforted because they safely got over the river, and had such glorious companions to attend them.

The talk that they had with the shining ones was about the glory of the place; who told them that the beauty and glory of it was inexpressible. There, said they, is the Mount Sion, the heavenly Jerusalem, the innumerable company of angels, and the spirits of just men made perfect. You are going now, said they, to the paradise of God, wherein you shall see the tree of life, and eat of the never-fading fruits thereof: and when you come there you shall have white robes given you, and your walk and talk shall be every day with the King, even all the days of eternity. There you shall not see again such things as you saw when you were in the lower region upon the earth: to wit, sorrow, sickness, affliction and death; For the former things are passed away. The men then asked, What must we do in the holy place? To whom it was answered, You must there receive the comfort of all your toil, and have joy for all your sorrow; you must reap what you have sown, even the fruit of all your prayers, and tears, and sufferings for the King by the way. In that place you must wear crowns of gold, and enjoy the perpetual sight and visions of the Holy One; for there you shall see Him as He is. There also you shall serve him continually.

John Bunyan

In an ancient legend, Pilate's wife is said to be standing by the Cross on the afternoon of Good Friday. She turns to the Centurion and says: 'Do you think Jesus is dead?'

'No, Lady, I don't', is the answer.

'Then, where is He?'

'Let loose in all the world, Lady, where neither Roman nor Jew nor any other man can stop the victory of His Risen Life.'

Olive Wyon

In terms of this world, the work of Jesus consisted only of scattered fragments. He moved from town to town, doing some work here and some work there.

Sent into the world to rescue the millions of mankind, to bring the whole earth back to God, His work in the end amounted to a number of separated bits and pieces – each thing in itself of course worthwhile, but without any apparent cohesion, a number of individual works performed on a number of different days in a number of different places, scattered and divided by time and distance, without any perfection of wholeness or integration.

But in the resurrection of Jesus, God took these bits and pieces of a disjointed ministry and wove from them a single garment of salvation for the whole world. The many and various things which Jesus did in Galilee and Judea were not lost. They were raised with Him on the first Easter morning, seen now to form one perfect pattern of redemption which was henceforward to adorn the heavenly world for ever. In the resurrection, they were gathered up into eternity. They were recovered and secured for ever.

But Christians have been made partakers of Christ's resurrection, and this means that for them as for Him, nothing in human life is lost or left behind.

These things, taken up into the manhood of Christ and raised with Him, form the stones of which the New Jerusalem is being built – the city which hath foundations, whose builder and maker is God. And in that celestial city all the fragmentary experiences of love and joy and peace and beauty, which, as we know them on earth, have ever their hands upon their lips bidding adieu, will be gathered together into one eternal moment of radiant beatitude.

Harry Williams

When you chose Me
You were made Mine; and I am yours for ever.
That which you gave, you have. All you who choose
To bear with Me the bitter burden of things
In patience, or, being burdened without choice,
Choose only to be patient, whether you give
Your bodies to be burned, your hearts to be broken,
Or only stand and wait in the market place
For work or bread in a long tediousness,
Think, it is I that stand and suffer with you,
Adding my innocence to redeem your guilt,
And yours with Mine, to ransom all mankind.
This is my courtesy, to make you partners
With God in your own rescue, nor do anything
But by your love and by your will consenting.
Come then, and take again your own sweet will
That once was buried in the spicy grave
With me, and now is risen with Me, more sweet
Than myrrh and cassia; come, receive again
All your desires, but better than your dreams,
All your lost loves, but lovelier than you knew,
All your fond hopes, but higher than your hearts
Could dare to frame them; all your City of God
Built by your faith, but nobler than you planned.
Instead of your justice, you shall have charity;

Instead of your happiness you shall have joy;
Instead of your peace the emulous exchange
Of love; and I will give you the morning star.

Dorothy Sayers

In a word, the story of Jesus, especially of his death and
resurrection, told years afterwards to those who never
met him, affected them in exactly the same way as the
resurrection had affected the broken and hopeless companions of Jesus at the beginning. The resurrection of Jesus
was, and is, still going on, both as a personal encounter
with Jesus as the Lord, the Living One, and as a coming-
to-life on the part of the hearers. The one follows from
the other, so that St Paul can speak about people being
'brought to life with Christ, even when we were dead in
our sins' and of being 'raised up together with Christ Jesus'
(Ephesians 2: 5, 6).

John V. Taylor

EASTER

Rise heart; thy Lord is risen. Sing his praise
                    Without delayes,
Who takes thee by the hand, that thou likewise
                    With him mayst rise:
that, as his death calcined thee to dust,
His life may make thee gold, and much more, just.

Awake, my lute, and struggle for thy part
                    With all thy art.
The crosse taught all wood to resound his name,
                    Who bore the same.
His stretched sinews taught all strings, what key
Is best to celebrate this most high day.

Consort both heart and lute, and twist a song
                              Pleasant and long:
Or, since all musick is but three parts vied
                              And multiplied,
O let thy blessed Spirit bear a part,
And make up our defects with his sweet art.

I got me flowers to straw thy way;
I got me boughs off many a tree:
But thou wast up by break of day,
And brought'st thy sweets along with thee.

The Sunne arising in the East,
Though he give light, & th' East perfume;
If they should offer to contest
With thy arising, they presume.

Can there be any day but this,
Though many sunnes to shine endeavour?
We count three hundred, but we misse:
There is but one, and that one ever.

                                        George Herbert

The everlasting ground, the historical expression, the contemporary presence, and all these of necessity co-existent.
This is an adequate working account of God for us, simply
because until Time and Space are done away it logically
exhausts the ways in which we can receive the personal
relationship which he offers us.

   But once we grasp this, God the Holy Spirit, so far from
being an awkward extra, becomes the dominant divine
fact in our lives. For if he is indeed, as trinitarian theology
insists, the fullness of God; and if he is that fullness in its
contemporary presence, then all our relations with God
come through him. It is him with whom we deal all the
time. As St Paul so penetratingly saw, if we say *Abba* it is
in him: the Father's everlasting arms are real to us because
he makes them so. If we know Jesus, it is because he makes
Jesus a living presence to us.

   That God, whom no man hath seen at any time, should

be to us not just an abstract idea but a Father; and that a Palestinian holy man of nearly two thousand years ago should be not just a historical character but a daily friend; are not these things miracles which we fail to recognise as such only because they are so familiar?

John Austin Baker

There is a way of winning by losing, a way of victory in defeat which we are going to discover.

L. van der Post

How fair and lovely is the hope which the Lord gave to the dead when he lay down like them beside them. Rise up and come forth and sing praise to him who has raised you from destruction.

Syrian Liturgy

I climb a secret hill
Each Easter morn;
Not for to breathe my fill
Of wonder born
Anew on such a day;
But, more to hear
A trump immortal sound
Within mine ear,
A noise of viols
And a beat of drums,
Bugles that cry,
'He did not die
For aye;
Behold he comes,
Victor from death's
Red fray.'

Alistair Maclean

Christ it is that sustains you and calls you to dwell with Him. Laugh at the threats of disease, despise the blows of misfortune, care not for the dark grave, and go forth at Christ's summons, for Christ will be to each man a kingdom, a light, a life, a crown.

Edward Harman, 1569
Burford Church

And he shall be as the light of the morning, when the sun riseth, even a morning without clouds; as the tender grass springing out of the earth by clear shining after rain.

2 Samuel 23: 4

As the moorland pool images the sun, so in our hours of self-giving thou shinest on us, and we mirror thee to men. But of the other land, our heaven to be, we have no picture at all. Only we know that thou art there. And Jesus the door and the welcome of each faithful one.

Alistair Maclean

Beloved, go and live thy life in the spirit of my dying,
    in righteousness and love;
Then truly shalt thou share my victory and taste my peace.

Hebridean Altars

Lord Jesus Christ,
alive and at large in the world,
help me to follow and find you there today,
in the places where I work,
meet people,
spend money,
and make plans.

Take me as a disciple of your kingdom,
to see through your eyes,
and hear the questions you are asking,
to welcome all others with your trust and truth,
and to change the things that contradict God's love,
by the power of the cross
and the freedom of your Spirit.
Amen.

John V. Taylor

FRESH SPRINGS

That perfect balance
Between agony and joy
Given
Through His Cross and Resurrection.
The loving touch
Of His hands
Heals
Our wounded hearts and spirits
Making them whole.
His loving patience
With us,
His compassion for us
Blesses us
With fresh springs of love:
Unutterable joy.

Society of the Sacred Cross

Alfred the Great translates Boethius:

It is the eternal cry of the clay to the potter, 'Why hast
Thou made me thus?' He will translate it, and after many
days he will translate the answer, which is no answer in
logic, but in excess of light.

'O Father, give the spirit power to climb
To the fountain of all light, and be purified.
Break through the mists of earth, the weight of the clod,
Shine forth in splendour, Thou that art calm weather,
And quiet resting place for faithful souls.
To see Thee is the end and the beginning,
Thou carriest us, and thou dost go before,
Thou art the journey, and the journey's end.'

translated by Helen Waddell

8

GET GOING

After the shock of bad news and the immediate numbness of any serious loss comes the long journey when the world seems strange and unsafe and our feelings confused and purposeless. Emergence into acceptance of a new way of living, particularly after a major bereavement, feels like recovery from illness. This may also be true of coming to terms with disability. I have therefore given my last section a challenging title because it is in taking up a new commitment to life as it is now that healing and liberation finally begin to break through. And it may only be a tentative beginning, with frequent lapses into much earlier states of mind. This is natural and does not mean there is no progress.

As John Taylor says in his prayer, making the break may feel like another death in itself. Mary Craig writes of a time limit, which must be different for each person, but the move onwards with 'the widened heart' is made easier by gratitude and the realization that new growth is springing up. Like Viktor Frankl, it may come only step by step.

The two short but important comments from Martin Buber were discovered during a lonely time in a big city. A few words in prose or poetry have always helped me gain a sense of perspective and recognition of the immense gains that can come through loss. For me such words have often been the singing bird of the Chinese proverb as well as a way into silence.

A prayer and a poem come from enclosed communities, places where isolation enlarges a deep sharing with the world outside.

I finish with the traditional Gaelic blessing of peace. The quiet earth and the shining stars can often bring us to the Son of Peace and our final homecoming.

I will set my face to the wind and scatter my handful of seed on high.

Arab proverb

I believe in the sun even when it is not shining.

I believe in love even when I feel it not.

I believe in God even when He is silent.

The above lines were found written on the walls of a cellar in Germany at the end of the Second World War.

Father,
If the hour has come
to make the break,
help me not to cling,
even though it feels like death.
Give me the inward strength
of my Redeemer, Jesus Christ,
to lay down this bit of life
and let it go,
so that I and others may be free
to take up whatever new and fuller life
you have prepared for us,
now and hereafter.
Amen.

John V. Taylor

When disaster first makes its unwelcome appearance into our lives, self-pity is the first, unavoidable, normal and probably right reaction. Courage flies out at the window, the world seems all of a sudden hostile and menacing, an alien place where we are no longer at home. We feel as though we are falling apart, and are deaf to everything but the shriek of our own misery. In the early stages I don't see how it is possible to fight self-pity. We only exhaust ourselves in trying to keep it at bay. But there is a time limit, and we alone can fix it. I believe it is possible to recognise the point of no return, the moment when self-pity threatens to become malignant. And that is when we have to stand firm, for if once we allow it to get a real hold we are doomed. Self-pity is a cancer which erodes not only our courage and our will to happiness, but also our humanity and our capacity to love. It destroys us, and it destroys the friends who love us and who want to help. After all, if we come to see ourselves as the ill-used victims of outrageous fate, all our actions and thoughts will be governed by bitterness, rancour and sour envy.

In the normal rush and hullabaloo of life, we have neither time nor mind for personal stock-taking. It is only when we are brought up short, when we are afraid or bewildered or disoriented, that we turn to God with an uncomprehending, frequently agnostic, cry for help. The bubble of our self-esteem has been pricked, our complacency has gone, and we are totally vulnerable. Then and only then can grace begin to operate in us, when we begin to take stock of ourselves, and to listen to our inner voices.

Is it really paradoxical that when we are distressed we turn to the friend who knows what distress can be like? We don't quite know why, but there doesn't seem much point in going for sympathy, the deep-down, understanding kind, to those other friends whose paths have always been smooth. It is as though human beings lack a whole dimension and cannot come to maturity until they have faced sorrow. There is an old Arab proverb which says 'Too much sunshine makes a desert' and the human heart is very often a desert. But sorrow irrigates the desert. A few years ago a friend of mine, a poet, stricken by the death of a close friend, wrote:

Shall I complain
How swift you passed?
Could I regret the widened heart?
Could I complain of it at all?

Mary Craig

THE CHOICE

If we could hang all our sorrows on pegs and were allowed
to choose those we liked best, everyone of us would take
back his own, for all the rest would seem even more
difficult to bear.

Martin Buber

———

Lord, I come before You surrounded by the members of
the community in which I live. I share my happiness with
them and it becomes greater. I share my troubles with
them and they seem smaller. May I never be too mean to
given, nor too proud to receive, for in giving and receiving
I discover You, and begin to understand the meaning of
life.

Let me not separate myself from the true strength of my
community: the experience and wisdom of old people, the
hopes of the young, and the examples of care and courage
which sustain me. Give me an open heart and an open
mind to welcome those who need me, and to receive Your
presence in my daily life.

I think of what we could be and the harmony and
friendship that could unite us. I think of our loneliness
and the friendships that could fill our lives. I think of the
good that we could do if we were one in spirit. I know
that this is Your will and pray for Your help. May I and
those around me find our joy together, and bless You for
the power You gave us to help each other.   Amen.

Forms of Prayer for Jewish Worship

By the hungry I will
                feed you
By the poor make you
                rich
By the broken
                I will mend you
Tell me which one is which

Pete Seeger
from a Christmas card

IN WATER

Question: It is written in Proverbs: 'As in water face
answereth to face, so the heart of man to man.' Why does
the verse read 'in water' and not 'in a mirror?'

Answer: Man can see his reflection in water only when he
bends close to it, and the heart of man too must lean down
to the heart of his fellow; then it will see itself within his
heart.

Martin Buber

ENOUGH

Matins is over, then. I hear
The sermon silence give, at last.
They rise to music, but appear
To find it taken a shade fast.
Still onward, out of step, they plod,
        Until 'O God
Our help in ages past' is past.

The seesaw hymn, the rasping psalm
Have stretched bucolic hands to shed
(More moving as their gift) some balm
Where this humped, eye-bright quilt is spread;
As though the form in this deep cot
        Were you, and not
Your clothes deceptive in your bed.

Dear one, the time is long, and yet
Not rugged, rather smooth than rough.
I love to tell you this, who set
My good before all ends. The stuff
Of life is coloured by your love,
        And still can prove
Pleasant enough, pleasant enough.

Laurence Whistler

IT WAS HERE

Beech-boles grope with muscular arms of darkness
Crossing out brightness from their own luminous leaves,
The leaves that are strong as faith in their maysilk weakness:
They move only as the fingertips of a dancer
Who balancing on the points of a chord achieves
Perpetual repose. On black shadow for ground
The wind-flowers burn with a light denser, intenser,
Just because the negation of all light is so near –
Surely it was here you stopped when the clue was found,
Watchful with morning eyes where the clearing widens
Into an absolute shining, surely it was here
You saw beyond the riddle the withheld solution?
Twenty and one years deep in the loam of silence,
Silent you stay. Why am I filled with elation?

Laurence Whistler

———

Always keep a green branch in your heart, and one day a
bird will come and perch on it and sing for you.

Chinese proverb

Spirit of God
Lord and Giver of Life,
moving between us and around,
like wind or water or fire
breathe into us your freshness that we may awake;

cleanse our vision that we may see more clearly;
kindle our senses that we may feel more sharply;
and give us the courage to live
as you would have us live,
through Jesus Christ our Lord,
Amen.

John V. Taylor

They are happy who are at peace with themselves.
  To begin with oneself, but not to end with
    oneself;
  To start from oneself, but not to aim at
    oneself;
  To comprehend oneself, but not to be preoccupied
    with oneself

Martin Buber
Forms of Prayer for Jewish Worship

We know God so little. We have formed innumerable
ideas of God and thought out innumerable names for him.
Sometimes we are afraid that he is none of these. But we
know our brethren better. It is easier for us to speak about
them. If we do so, perhaps we shall catch a better glimpse
of our incarnate God than by means of concepts and ideas.
Our brethren are God's messengers in the mysterious sense
that they bear the author of the message within them, and,
what is more, are that author himself.

Ladislaus Boros

GROWING UP

Time has changed me.
Once I thought to win
Some camouflage from prying eyes
That scratch for flaws within
And call them sin:
    Now I don't fear.

Time controlled me
When I thought I could
Don armour for the ones I loved;
Believing if I should
I did them good:
    It does not wear.

Then time enticed me,
Coveting relief,
To stand behind these friends of mine
And working at their grief
To play the thief:
    I now don't dare.

And time has left me
Like an empty stage
On which the ones my care is for
In loving or in rage
Can come of age:
    This is like prayer.

Source unknown

One day, a few days after the liberation, I walked through the country past flowering meadows, for miles and miles, toward the market town near the camp. Larks rose to the sky and I could hear their joyous song. There I stopped, looked around, and up to the sky – and then I went down on my knees. At that moment there was very little I knew of myself or of the world – I had but one sentence in mind – always the same 'I called to the Lord from my narrow prison and He answered me in the freedom of space'.

How long I knelt there and repeated this sentence memory can no longer recall. But I know that on that day, in that hour, my new life started. Step for step I progressed, until I again became a human being.

Viktor Frankl

See yourself in the presence of God, and in the presence of all the angels and saints. Join with them in worshipping God, saying Holy, Holy, Holy.

Next be silent, and consider that all the glory of God is love which streams down upon all His creation; so that now He is looking down upon you with the most intimate and loving care, and all those angels and saints are sharing in that loving regard by interceding for you.

Finally, after allowing yourself to be bathed in that love, make a very simple, earnest and humble petition for grace to understand more fully, and to respond more worthily to, this immense love of God.

Philip Loyd

BEING VISITED BY A FRIEND DURING ILLNESS

I have been ill so long that I do not count the days;
    At the southern window, evening – and again evening.
Sadly chirping in the grasses under my eaves
The winter sparrows morning and evening sing.
By an effort I rise and lean heavily on my bed;
Tottering I step towards the door of the courtyard.
By chance I meet a friend who is coming to see me;
Just as if I had gone specially to meet him.

They took my couch and placed it in the setting sun;
    They spread my rug and I leaned on the balcony-pillar.
Tranquil talk was better than any medicine;
Gradually the feelings came back to my numbed heart.

translated by Arthur Waley

————

There is one who sings the song of his own soul, and in his soul he finds everything, full spiritual satisfaction.

And there is one who sings the song of the people. For he does not find the circle of his private soul wide enough, and so goes beyond it, reaching for more powerful heights. And he unites himself with the soul of the community of

Israel, sings its songs, suffers with its sorrows and is delighted by its hopes . . .

And there is one whose soul lifts beyond the limitations of Israel to sing the song of mankind. His spirit expands to include the glory of the human image and its dreams . . .

And there is one who lifts beyond this level, until he becomes one with all creation and all creatures, and all the worlds. And with all of them he sings a song . . .

And there is one who rises together with the bundle of all these songs. All of them sing out, each gives meaning and life to the other.

And this completeness is the song of holiness, the song of God, the song of Israel . . .

Rav Kook
Forms of Prayer for Jewish Worship

MY LORD GOD,

I have no idea where I am going. I do not see the road ahead of me. I cannot know for certain where it will end. Nor do I really know myself, and the fact that I think that I am following your will does not mean that I am actually doing so. But I believe that the desire to please you does in fact please you. And I hope I have that desire in all that I am doing. I hope that I will never do anything apart from that desire. And I know that if I do this you will lead me by the right road though I may know nothing about it. Therefore I will trust you always though I may seem to be lost and in the shadow of death. I will not fear, for you are ever with me, and you will never leave me to face my perils alone.

Thomas Merton
from Gethsemane Monastery

COMMUNITY

It is as if the rhythm
  Of flight has steadied:
A sure sweep of wings;
Flight of heart as well as of mind,
Carries one out of the disturbed air
  Strengthened
Having learnt to trust oneself to others;
Not thrusting them away
  When the cold dark air chills,
  But resting on their wings.
We share flight upheld by the wings
  Of His Spirit
  And wake singing.

from Tymawr Convent

Deep Peace of the Running Wave to you
Deep Peace of the Flowing Air to you
Deep Peace of the Quiet Earth to you
Deep Peace of the Shining Stars to you
Deep Peace of the Son of Peace to you.

Traditional Gaelic

INDEX OF SOURCES AND ACKNOWLEDGEMENTS

The editor acknowledges with gratitude the courtesy of the following companies and individuals.

INTRODUCTION

BEDE JARRETT, Prayer from Syon Abbey, South Brent, Devon.

GOLLINTZER, H., KUBER, K., SCHNEIDER, R. (eds), *Dying we Live. The final messages and records of some Germans who defied Hitler*. London, Fontana Books, 1958.

MONAHAN, J. A. (ed.), *Before I Sleep . . . The Last Days of Dr Tom Dooley*. New York, Farras, Strauss & Cudaby, 1961.

NOUWEN, H. J. M., *The Wounded Healer*. New York, Doubleday & Co., 1972.

BAKER, J. A., *The Foolishness of God*. London, Darton, Longman & Todd, 1970.

1   THE SEARCH FOR MEANING

THORNBOROUGH, P., 'A Prayer', in *New Christian*, 2 April 1970.

WADDELL, H. (tr.), *Lyrics from the Chinese*. London, Constable, 1943.

WADDELL, H. (tr.), *Poetry in the Dark Ages*. (The Eighth W. P. Ker Memorial Lecture, University of Glasgow, 1947.) London, Constable, 1958.

'Memorial Service for the Six Million', in *Forms of Prayer for Jewish Worship, Vol. 1, Daily and Sabbath Prayerbook*. The Reform Synagogues of Great Britain, 1977.

FRANKL, V., *Man's Search for Meaning*. London, Hodder & Stoughton, 1964.

HENKE, E., a patient in St Christopher's Hospice.

HAYLOCK EYRE, J., a patient in St Christopher's Hospice.

VAN KAAM, A., *Spirituality and the Gentle Life*. New Jersey, Dimension Books Inc., 1974.

BAKER, J. A., *The Whole Family of God*. London and Oxford, Ward Lock, a division of Cassell Publishers Ltd, 1981.

2 ANGER

KUSHNER, H. S., *When Bad Things Happen to Good People*. London, Pan Books, 1982.

'Zohar' and 'Chasidic' in *Forms of Prayer for Jewish Worship, Vol. 1, Daily and Sabbath Prayerbook*. The Reform Synagogues of Great Britain, 1977.

DOMINIAN, J., quoted in Priestland, G., *Priestland's Progress*. London, BBC Publications, 1981.

CLEMENTS, B., in *The Unity Book of Prayers*. London, Geoffrey Chapman, a division of Cassell Publishers Ltd, 1969.

PRESCOTT, H. F. M., *The Man on A Donkey: A Chronicle*. New York, Macmillan, 1952.

LEWIS, C. S., *Reflections on the Psalms*. London, Geoffrey Bles, 1958.

TRIMAKAS sj, K. A. (tr.), *Prayers written by Lithuanian Prisoners in Northern Siberia*. New York, Paulist Press, 1960.

POPE JOHN PAUL II, reported in *The Times*, June 1982.

BAKER, J. A., *Travels in Oudamovia*. Leighton Buzzard, Faith Press, 1976.

LLOYD, R., *The Borderland*. London, George Allen & Unwin, 1960.

HERBERT, G., 'Love (III)' in *The Works of George Herbert*. Oxford, Oxford University Press, 1941.

PRIESTLAND, G., *Priestland's Progress*. London, BBC Publications, 1981. By permission of BBC Enterprises Ltd.

MACLEAN, A., in Reith, M., *God in Our Midst*. London, SPCK, 1975.

DAWSON, B., in Saunders, C. (ed.), *St Christopher's in Celebration*. London, Hodder & Stoughton, 1988.

3 SUFFERING

TEILHARD DE CHARDIN, in Braybrooke, N. (ed.), *The Wind and the Rain*. London, Secker & Warburg, 1962.

TORRIE, M., *Selected Poems*. Richmond, Cruse, 1979. By permission of the author.

LEVI YITZCHAK OF BERDITCHEV, in *Forms of Prayer for Jewish Worship, Vol. 1, Daily and Sabbath Prayerbook*. The Reform Synagogues of Great Britain, 1977.

TRIMAKAS SJ, K. A. (tr.), *Prayers written by Lithuanian Prisoners in Northern Siberia*. New York, Paulist Press, 1960.

APPLETON, G., *One Man's Prayers*. London, SPCK, 1967.

BAKER, J. A., *Travels in Oudamovia*. Leighton Buzzard, Faith Press, 1976.

SAYERS, D. L., 'The Just Vengeance' in *Four Sacred Plays*. London, Gollancz, 1948. By permission of David Higham Assoc. Ltd.

BAKER, J. A., *The Foolishness of God*. London, Darton, Longman & Todd, 1970.

CATHERINE OF SIENA, in Wyon, O., *Consider Him: Three Meditations on the Passion Story*. London, SCM Press, 1956.

WARRICK, G. (ed.), *Revelations of Divine Love*. London, Methuen, 1901.

MOULE, H. C. G., *Christus Consolator*. London, SPCK, 1931.

MILNER-WHITE, E., *A Procession of Passion Prayers*. London, SPCK, 1956.

TAYLOR, J. V., 'Christmas Venite' in *A Christmas Sequence and other Poems*. Oxford, The Amate Press, 1989.

PRESCOTT, H. F. M., *The Man on a Donkey: A Chronicle*. New York, Macmillan, 1952.

4 DYING

SMITH, S., *The Collected Poems of Stevie Smith*, Penguin. By permission of James MacGibbon.

LAWRENCE, D. H., *Selected Poems* (Viking Compass edition). New York, Viking Press, 1959.

BUNYAN, J., *The Pilgrim's Progress*.

Clergyman's widow, in Blythe, R., *The View in Winter: Reflections on Old Age*. London, Allen Lane, 1979.

GOLDIN, G., 'Winter Rise' in *Poems of Aging*. Patten Press, 66 Hayle Terrace, Hayle, Cornwall, 1981.

An Isleman, in Reith, M., *God in our Midst*. London, SPCK, 1975.

CARRETTO, C., *I, Francis: The Spirit of St Francis of Assisi*. London, Collins, 1982.

THORNTON WILDER, *The Bridge of San Luis Rey*.

REEMAN, S., a patient in St Christopher's Hospice. 'Murmurings' and 'Lost Property' appear in *St Christopher's in Celebration*. London, Hodder & Stoughton, 1988.

CONGREVE, Fr, in Wyon, O., *Consider Him: Three Meditations on the Passion Story*. London, SCM Press, 1956.

CELAN, P., in *Forms of Prayer for Jewish Worship, Vol. 1, Daily and Sabbath Prayerbook*. The Reform Synagogues of Great Britain, 1977.

Traditional Gaelic, in Reith, M., *God in Our Midst*. London, SPCK, 1975.

TEILHARD DE CHARDIN, *Le Milieu Divin*. London, Collins, 1957.

DRAKE, M., a patient in St Christopher's Hospice.

BAKER, J. A., *The Foolishness of God*. London, Darton, Longman & Todd, 1970.

DAWSON, B., in Saunders, C. (ed.), *St Christopher's in Celebration*. London, Hodder & Stoughton, 1988.

HASKINS, M., source unknown.

COMPER, F. M. M., source unknown.

5   GONE AWAY

THOMAS À KEMPIS, *The Imitation of Christ*.

MASEFIELD, J., *The Midnight Folk*. London, Heinemann, 1957. By permission of the Society of Authors as the literary representative of the Estate of John Masefield.

'Prayer in the Home before a Funeral' in *Forms of Prayer for Jewish Worship, Vol. 1, Daily and Sabbath Prayerbook*. The Reform Synagogues of Great Britain, 1977.

APPLETON, G., *The Word is the Seed: Meditations starting from the Bible*. London, SPCK, 1976.

BOROS, L., *We are Future*. London, Search Press, 1971.

HOPKINS, G. M., *Poems*. Oxford, Oxford University Press, 1967.

WADDELL, H. (tr.), *Poetry in the Dark Ages* (The Eighth W. P. Ker

Memorial Lecture, University of Glasgow, 1947.) London, Constable, 1958.

APPLETON, G., *One Man's Prayers*. London, SPCK, 1967.

Traditional Gaelic, in Reith, M., *God in our Midst*. London, SPCK, 1975.

WADDELL, H. (tr.), *Mediaeval Latin Lyrics* (2nd edn.). London, Constable, 1933.

6 LEFT BEHIND

ALLINGHAM, M., *The Tiger in the Smoke*. Harmondsworth, Penguin Books, 1957.

WALEY, A. (tr.), *Chinese Poems*, London, George Allen & Unwin, 1946.

TRAPNELL, B. M. W., personal communication.

KUSHNER, H., *When Bad Things Happen to Good People*. London, Pan Books, 1982.

FRANKL, V., *Man's Search for Meaning*. London, Hodder & Stoughton, 1964.

LENEY, N., *In a Lifetime. A Collection of poems*. New York, J. N. R. Publishing, 1975.

Forms of Prayer for Jewish Worship, Vol. 1, Daily and Sabbath Prayerbook. The Reform Synagogues of Great Britain, 1977.

MOULE, H. C. G., *Christus Consolator. Words for hearts in trouble*. London, SPCK, 1931.

HARVEY, N. P., *Death's Gift. Chapters on Resurrection and Bereavement*. London, Epworth Press, 1985.

BONHOEFFER, D., *Letters and Papers from Prison*. London, SCM Press, 1953.

BLAKE, W., 'Several questions answered', *Collected Poems*.

HOLM, A., *I am David*. London, Methuen, 1965.

VAUGHAN, H., *The Works of Henry Vaughan*. Oxford, Clarendon Press, 1914.

BAKER, J. A., *The Whole Family of God*. London & Oxford, Ward Lock, a division of Cassell Publishers Ltd, 1981.

LANGE, M., a patient in St Christopher's Hospice.

LINDBERGH, A. M., *Hour of Gold, Hour of Lead. Diaries and Letters 1929–32*. New York & London, Harcourt Brace Jovanovich, 1973.

7   RESURRECTION

BUNYAN, J., *The Pilgrim's Progress.*

WYON, O., *Consider Him: Three Meditations on the Passion Story.* London, SCM Press, 1956.

WILLIAMS, H., *Jesus and the Resurrection.* London, Ward Lock, a division of Cassell Publishers Ltd, 1961.

SAYERS, D. L., 'The Just Vengeance' in *Four Sacred Plays.* London, Gollancz, 1948.

TAYLOR, J. V., *A Matter of Life and Death.* London, SCM Press, 1986.

HERBERT, G., 'Easter' in *The Works of George Herbert.* Oxford, Clarendon Press, 1941.

BAKER, J. A., 'Father of the Poor' in *Christian*, Vol. 2, 30, 1974.

VAN DER POST, L., *A Bar of Shadow.* London, Hogarth Press, 1954.

Syrian Liturgy, from Grail leaflets.

MACLEAN, A., in Reith, M., *God in our Midst.* London, SPCK, 1975.

HARMAN, E., from a tablet in Burford Parish Church, 1569.

Hebridean Altars, in Reith, M., *God in Our Midst.* London, SPCK, 1975.

Society of the Sacred Cross, from a card (anonymous).

WADDELL, H. (tr.), *Poetry in the Dark Ages.* (The Eighth W. P. Ker Memorial Lecture, University of Glasgow, 1947.) London, Constable, 1958.

8   GET GOING

TAYLOR, J. V., *A Matter of Life and Death.* London, SCM Press, 1986.

CRAIG, M., *Blessings, an Autobiographical Fragment.* London, Hodder & Stoughton, 1979.

BUBER, M., *Ten Rungs: Hasidic Sayings collected and edited.* New York, Schocken Books, 1962.

Forms of Prayer for Jewish Worship, Vol. 1, Daily and Sabbath Prayerbook, The Reform Synagogues of Great Britain, 1977.

WHISTLER, L., *To Celebrate Her Living.* London, Rupert Hart-Davis, 1967.

BOROS, L., *We are Future.* London, Search Press, 1971.

FRANKL, V., *Man's Search for Meaning*. London, Hodder & Stoughton, 1964.

LOYD, P., *The Life According to St John. Eighty-four Meditations*. London, Ward Lock, a division of Cassell Publishers Ltd, 1936.

WALEY, A. (tr.), *Chinese Poems*. London, George Allen & Unwin, 1946.

MERTON, THOMAS, prayer published by Gethsemane Monastery. Society of the Sacred Cross, from a card (unpublished).

Some of the material in this book previously appeared in *Beyond All Pain* edited by Cicely Saunders and published by SPCK.